MEMORIALS, NIGHTSC.

ANTHONY HIRST was born in Huddersfield, Yorkshire in 1945. He was educated at Ashville College Harrogate, and Emmanuel College Cambridge. He had a very varied career as library assistant, furniture maker, building contractor, architectural designer and postman, before returning to university in 1992, obtaining an MA in Byzantine Studies and PhD in Modern Greek Literature at King's College London, after which he was a research fellow at Princeton University and then at Queen's University Belfast, where he was later a lecturer in Byzantine and Modern Greek. He is course director of the International Byzantine Greek Summer School, now at Trinity College Dublin.

He is the author of *God and the poetic ego: the appropriation of biblical and liturgical language in the poetry of Palamas, Sikelianos and Elytis* (Peter Lang, 2004); editor and translator of *These scattered isles: Alonnisos and the Lesser Northern Sporades* by Kóstas Mavríkis (Oxford Maritime Research, 2010); and editor of *Alexandria, real and imagined* (with Michael Silk, Ashgate Publishing, 2004), *The Ionian Islands: aspects of their history and culture* (with Patrick Sammon, Cambridge Scholars Publishing, 2014), the journal *Basilissa: Belfast, Byzantium and beyond* (2004), and *Sweet-voiced Sappho, The Golden Face* and *Viral Verse* for Colenso Books (see below). He has re-edited, or "de-edited" as he prefers to say, the Greek text of the main body of Cavafy's poetry for the Oxford World's Classics series (C. P. Cavafy, *The collected poems*, Oxford University Press, 2007). He has published many articles on modern Greek literature (especially the poetry of Cavafy).

OTHER POETRY VOLUMES FROM COLENSO BOOKS

Sweet-voiced Sappho: some of the extant poems of Sappho of Lesbos and other Ancient Greek poems, translated by Theodore Stephanides, edited by Anthony Hirst (2015).

The fruitful discontent of the word: a further selection of poems by Lawrence Durrell, edited by Peter Baldwin (2018, in conjunction with The Delos Press).

Yannis Ritsos among his contemporaries: twentieth-century Greek poetry, translated by Marjorie Chambers (2018).

Στων Κυκλώπων τη Χώρα (In the Land of the Cyclopes) by Iakovos Menelaou, with an introduction by Patrick Sammon (2018, in Greek only).

Το Χρυσό Προσωπείο / The Golden Face by Theodore Stephanides, with Greek translation by Vera Konidari, edited by Anthony Hirst (2019).

Reading the signs by Jim Potts (2020).

Viral verse: pandemic poems and images, edited by Anthony Hirst (2020).

Memorials, nightscapes, etcetera

poems of several decades

by

ANTHONY HIRST

COLENSO BOOKS
2020

First published November 2020 by
Colenso Books
68 Palatine Road, London N16 8ST, U.K.
colensobooks@gmail.com

ISBN 978-1-912788-05-7

Versions of some of these poems have been published before, as follows: "Theatre of Dionysus, Athens" in *Πῶς λέγεις;* (magazine of the Department of Classics, King's College London), 1992/3; "Homecomings" in *Dialogos: Hellenic Studies Review* 4 (1997), p. 83; "In memoriam L.G.D." in *Deus Loci: The Lawrence Durrell Journal* NS7 (1999–2000), pp. 166–7; "Lunch on Poros" in *Deus Loci: The Lawrence Durrell Journal* NS15 (2016–2017), p. 129. Also, under the pseudonym Antony Mylonás: "The quick and the dead" in *Staple* 32 (Spring 1995), p. 75; "An old man at midnight mass" in *Acumen* 23 (September 1995), p. 6; "The Pilgrims' Way (postcards from Kent)" in *Rustic Rub* 5 (undated [winter 1995/96]), pp. 76–9; "A night out on Thasos" in *Oxford Poetry* IX.2 (Winter/Spring 1996), p. 80; "At an Oxford conference" in *A Blossom of Dreams*, ed. T. Piper (International Library of Poetry, London, 1998), p. 5.

The image on the front cover is the author's photograph
of the Nile near Luxor, from a hotel garden.

The image on the back cover is the author's photograph
of the family grave in its context in Salendine Nook
Baptist Cemetery, Huddersfied, Yorkshire, the location of poems
on pages 3–5, 27–29 and 46–49. The inscription on the headstone,
beginning with the word PEACE (clearly visible near the centre
of the image) is referred to in the poem on page 18.

For my children and my sister's children

ISABEL, AMOS, POLLY, OSSIE & DAISY

and for their children

ROSA, HARRY, AILSA, SCARLET,
ALBIE, OTIS, EFFI & DELLA

at present aged from twenty-seven to four,
some of whom may now
and others who may, years from now,
find things here to surprise,
inform, amuse, perplex, disturb
or even shock them.

And to the clear and sustaining memory
of my mother

MARGARET *(d. 1976)*

and my paternal grandfather

AMOS *(d. 1955)*

and to the less clear and unsettling memory
of my father

GEOFF *(d. 1950)*

who never knew
what became of his children.

v

CONTENTS

INTRODUCTION   xiii

Memorials

A photograph perhaps . . . a mask, a portrait even   3
Theatre of Dionysus, Athens   6
That afternoon   7
Homecomings   9
Greek mariners *or* The naming of craft   10
The secret beach   11
A classical dichotomy   12
Coincidence (1st of October 1991)   13
A royal dilemma   14
Poison on Poros   15
Dead friends   16
An old recording   18
War dead   19
In Salonica today the sea   20
At an Oxford conference   21
Still life, Sigh . . . gone   22
In the Commonwealth Cemetery at Souda   23
The last breakfast   24
The effects of alcohol   25
In memoriam L.G.D.   26
Here's to you, Ma!   27
. . . update on redevelopment (February 2019)
      with automotive digressions   27
. . . and twelve months later   29
Anna Palaiologou's gate   30
A mourning walk on a spring afternoon   31
Bashō, Oppenheimer, and a dream   33
Memorials (1941, 1989)   39

CONTENTS

Ka and Kavafis   42
The family plot, Salendine Nook Baptist Cemetery   46

Nightscapes, seascapes, lovescapes, landscapes . . .

Night conceits   53
Night out on Thasos   54
Attic power cut   54
Lunch on Poros   55
Saturday night and Sunday morning   56
"I do not think that they will sing to me"   57
Hearing the dawn   58
Dawn ferry   59
Riding at anchor   59
Aegean snapshots 7 x 5   60
When I arrived, one day years ago   62
Waking from dreams   64
Volcano days   65
Visitors   66
From the Manickam Tourist Home   67
Air India to JFK   68
Princeton porches   69
Cloudscapes   70
Monastic silences in Kefalonia   71
Hangovers   72
The railway station in Kampala   73
An Antique Valentine   74
Speculum, speculum *or* In my Lady's Chamber   75
Little deaths   77
Bodily comfort   78
Lilies of the valley   79
For a daughter born 12.45 a.m.   80
Remember me to him   81
Long ago   82
. . . and two generations later   82
Mouse poem for a child   83

Minoan royal prerogative 84
Autumn in Chania 85
Tomb of Antipatros, a Macedonian 86
An die ferne Geliebte 87
Anticipating spring 88
Sleeping, not leaping 89
Travelling alone 90
Familiar predicament 90
These places 91
TV in Vietnam in 2012 92
Platonic manikins, Athens 93
Hypertension 94
The difficult syntax of love 95
Plateia Varnava, Athens 96
The swallows of Kastoria 99
The quick and the dead 101
. . . and I, I lie alone 103
London winter evening: linked verse 104
The journey to Asine 106
Safari drive, Uganda 107
Mahoma Falls 108
At the Crater Lakes 109
Capitals 110
Preparations 111
Friend in despair 112
Nightmare 113
The Pilgrims' Way (postcards from Kent) 114

'twixt earnest & joke: poems for Alison's eyes

"The Muse was prescient" (untitled) 124
Loins and eyes 125
ἅλς ἰόνιος / hals ionios (Ionian Sea) 126
As on lips I fixed my gaze 127
So in Albania 128
Is an old Muse any less inspiring? 129

Sail on from Bougainvillea   130
O Snail!   131
So nail your courage to the sticking place . . .   132
Λάϊνος / Laïnos (Made of marble)   135
Σαλόνι / Salóni (Saloon)   137
Σα λιόντισσα, σα λιοντάρι / Sa lióndissa, sa liondári
    (Like a lioness, like a lion)   138
Η Άλισον της Τροίας / I Álison tis Trías
    (Alison of Troy)   139
Also in sleep   140
As in loving, so in Lagan's stream   141
In so late an hour   142
There is no laptop here   143
ἄλινος θήρα / alinos thera (a hunt without nets)   144
As I long   146
's I alone again?   147
As I only noted cursorily at first   149
In solaria   150
Ναι, σ' όλο τον κόσμο σε γυρεύω / Nai, s' ólo ton
    kósmo se yirévo (Yes, through all the world
    I seek for you)   151
No aisle for Alison?   155
Alison + I   156
Ars is longa, vita's brevis   157
Loans I never could repay   158
In a solitary deck chair   159
Travails on arrival and departure   161
Man losing his bearings   162
An' so I learn some home truths   163
This is a long-distance phone call   164
Lady Julian's offering   166

Remnants of religion

The hands of God   169
A mixed blessing   170

Klafthmonos Square, Athens, 25th of March 2001   171
Visitation   172
Strange land: a child's story   173
An old man at Midnight Mass   175
A Brief Guide to the Monastery of Daphni   176
To the Ayatolla Komeini: an oblique tribute   179
Ite missa est   182
That other city   184
Pins and needles   185
Preaching with precaution   186
Veni creator spiritus   186
A timetrick   187
Confusion   188
A hotel room in Chania   189
Ghosts   192
Unspoken   193
Dramatic fragment   193
The sick house   194
Behind the Veil   197
Good Friday in Herakleion   198
A kind of death   199
Holy Saturday   200
Easter Vigil   201
Cracks and hollows in the Rock of Ages   202
Sea voices   205
The silence of the icons   206

NOTES   211
INDEX OF TITLES AND FIRST LINES   249

INTRODUCTION

I had thought of calling this an Extradition rather than an Introduction. The majority of these poems are being hauled out for
the first time to face critical scrutiny in another country, that is to
say, by persons unknown to me. Only eight individual poems and
one sequence of twenty short poems ("The Pilgrims' Way") have
been published before (details on the Copyright page). Some
have been read by the persons they concern; others shown to a
small number of friends, colleagues or relations; some have been
aired at poetry readings in New York, Belfast and London.

The earliest of these "poems of several decades" belongs, I
think, to the winter of 1963–64 (my first year at Cambridge), the
latest to February 2020.

When I began to think about the organization of the poems,
the division into four sections soon became the obvious strategy.
Quite a number of my poems deal with the dead — family
members and others known to me personally, those killed in
wars, some fictional and some ancient dead. Such poems — not
all sombre — with a few others that don't concern the dead
constitute the first section, "Memorials".

Most varied and most extensive is the second section,
"Nightscapes, seascapes, lovescapes, landscapes . . .", where all
four terms and some other kinds of -scapes are represented,
though poems of night and love predominate.

The most narrowly defined section is the third, "'twixt earnest
& joke". It is the chronicle of a brief liaison, a three-month erotic
obsession, mostly constructed and conducted inside my head,
though it did involve considerable travelling and extensive email
correspondence. The thirty-three "half-humourous" and sometimes self-mocking poems end with a "revelation" whose effect is

the opposite of a religious conversion, leading into the last section, "Remnants of religion". This includes my quarrels, as a former Christian, with religion and the Bible, and, in some of the earlier poems — earlier in time, not in position in the book — my attempts to fill the gap left by what is conventionally called a "loss of faith". In this section there are several poems which emanate from recurrent periods of depression and confusion in my twenties, thirties and forties, and some odd short poems of a slightly abstract nature, not rooted in immediate experience.

Here and there, especially in the second section, the grouping of a few poems and the sequencing within such small groups is determined by autobiography, and the sequence of the poems in third section (described above as a "chronicle") is almost entirely determined by chronology; in the fourth section some groups of poems are arranged according to the ecclesiastical calendar. Otherwise, the poems move about from country to country and back and forth among the decades and the basic idea underlying the arrangement, while hard to define, is certainly not chronological either in terms of dates of writing or in terms of the dates of the events or circumstances which prompted the writing. The sequence is determined, rather, by the interaction of two conflicting principles: contrast, and thematic or tonal links between successive poems.

There are several poems in this book which employ a novel syllabic stanza (looser than the Japanese forms to which it is related). Its rules may be simply stated: 23 syllables (longer than the *haiku* but shorter than the *tanka*), divided into four lines, with no line shorter than three syllables or longer than nine, and without strong enjambment — line ends must coincide with at least minor syntactical divisions. It derives from a string of words that came to me entirely spontaneously and without context a very long time ago, probably in the late 1960s, and always stuck in my mind, now forming part of "London winter evening":

> Leave the warm ashes
> to their soundless dancing
> no use straining
> to hear the whispering of leaves.

It was only long afterwards, in the 1990s, that I thought to count the syllables in this fragment, and then to exploit the form, deciding on the rules outlined above.

About twenty-five years ago the poet and incisive critic David Ricks read and wrote detailed comments on some twenty of the poems with Greek connections. At the time I was a mature — or perhaps I should say "over-ripe" — student of modern Greek literature at King's College London and David was my PhD supervisor there. Part of the purpose of his scrutiny was to select poems which, with some revision, might be included in the then fairly new journal *Dialogos: Hellenic Studies Review*, of which he was a founding editor. One poem, "Homecomings", was indeed so published, although David had actually invited me to revise eleven poems for resubmission. I had not then, and still have not, been able to "stomach", to use his apt expression, some of the cuts which he advised. And some of the small excisions that he urged — short phrases, single words — in the interest of "compression" would have left me feeling that it was no longer quite my own voice. The excisions may well have made for better poems, but my voice is — or, rather, my voices are — perhaps more diffuse, more garrulous and prone to asides, less concise than his. Nevertheless a number of poems have been improved by his interventions, and for this I am profoundly grateful.

I am grateful too — for his encouragement — to another poet, Jim Potts, who read almost all of these poems during the preparation of this volume and whose indications of his favourites offered me some surprises. I would also like to thank

Maria Strani-Potts and Vera Konidari who corrected and commented on the one poem in Greek and Greek words or phrases in other poems or poem titles.

At the back of the book I have provided some rather extensive Notes. No one needs to read these notes — I mean no one should feel obliged to read them. So no one who does read them should feel offended at being told what they already know. Every reader has their own cultural background which may, in some cases, hardly overlap at all with that of an author they are reading. So the notes are primarily for those whose cultural background is different from mine. In particular, one cannot now assume (I am tempted to add "happily") even among readers in a nominally Christian country like the UK, any degree of familiarity with the Christian Bible, which happens to be a part of my cultural background (or "cultural baggage"). Unsurprisingly then, it is the fourth section, "Remnants of religion", which is most heavily annotated.

My initial reason for starting on those Notes was to acknowledge where I had deliberately used expressions taken from other writings. The most extensive instances of such borrowings are revealed in the notes to the poems "In memoriam L.G.D." and "To the Ayatollah Khomeini", and in the general note to the section "'twixt earnest and joke". The note to *hals ionios* (Ionian Sea)" provided an excuse for a short essay on a poem by Cavafy. In some of the notes I have in mind readers whose native language is other than English. Only occasionally do the notes provide indications of the personal background to a poem — for poetry is, after all, a form of fiction.

Anthony Hirst
Stoke Newington and Bossay-sur-Claise
2018–2020

Memorials

A photograph perhaps . . .
a mask, a portrait even

Two hundred miles on trains,
a damp November day,
to plant a few spring bulbs
in a plot of ground not even
two-feet square between
the flagstones on my mother's grave.
Unlikely I'll be back in time
to see the flowers, or they'll be seen
by anyone who knew the face
behind the name engraved here.
And yet, two hundred miles on trains,
a damp November day . . .

I came once — years ago —
in August, worried
that the rose had not survived
two hard winters of neglect.
Expecting only dead wood,
the profusion of its tiny flowers —
white, pink blushed —
sparked a confusion of memories
and I felt my mother in her younger days —
a photograph perhaps — a flowered dress
caught and ruffled by the wind —
spring up to greet me like a lover.

And even now, in mid November,
flowers remain, and some
still hold their colour,

as though they'd hung on, waiting
for my promised summer visit,
postponed until today, when,
as before, I sense her presence
who once inhabited this mouldy corpse
that nourishes maybe, if its roots
go deep enough, the rose —
the wild rose confined
within this narrow bed.

Later — not now, but tomorrow —
I must prune the rosebush ruthlessly,
reduce it to the wood. Not now,
as the day fades and tears mix
with the soft rain on my cheeks,
remembering how gently death took her
(who for half a lifetime
had had no lover); did not demand
she looked him in the face, for he'd
already sealed her eyes and freed
her vision from the confines of that room
and of the hours in which she lay there.

And when, about the middle of a day,
relieved of all responsibility,
she finally relaxed into his arms
(though we still held her hands),
it seemed a simple thing to die.
And later, sitting there, it came to me
that the face was no longer a face,
but a mask, a portrait even,
which the undertakers' skill had recomposed;

that the bed held merely a waxwork,
an image to which one might
light candles — nothing more.

And seeing the bright varnished box,
with its vulgar chrome handles,
lowered down between the grass-
like mats that hid the soil,
I felt no outrage (as I had with others),
knowing that in no sense was *she*
there, nor could anywhere be found
outside the boundaries of her life.
And yet, this plot of ground,
after fourteen years,
two hundred miles,
a damp November day . . .

Theatre of Dionysus, Athens

Forget all this is marble for a moment
and think of a company of travelling players,
who, like a circus troupe, take stage and seating with them.
You've arrived, say, in the lunch-break, and the theatre,
already half-dismantled — you can see the pieces
laid out in rows for loading — is deserted.
The actors (labourers today), who last night gave —
was it, perhaps, the world premiere of the *Oresteia*,
are down there, you imagine, resting in the shade
of cypresses and pines. They'll soon be back, you think,
to clear away the last few moulded panels
with their crouching satyrs seeming to support the stage,
the remaining tiers of benches; and to stack
the high-backed front-row chairs, marked with titles
of civil and religious dignitaries
(which can be changed of course to suit the needs
of any town they visit).
                 But they don't return —
only an officious youth, speaking, awkwardly,
your own barbarian tongue (neither his nor theirs)
orders a couple strayed inside the ropes to move.
And as you watch his mildly threatening approach,
their grudging exit, in the blinding heat
the centuries evaporate and all this transient wreckage,
abandoned by the actors, turns to stone.

That afternoon

I can see him now . . .
as I often saw him . . .
as he must have been that afternoon.
An old man, certainly, and frail,
but tall still, unbowed
by the years, or the loss.

The skin of his face
still taut, and the few
strands of silver hair
carefully combed across
the polished scalp.
Sitting at ease in his wide armchair —
green velvet, bright green it was.

Lace curtains scattering sunlight
over the heavy furniture
and the carpet with its sombre flowers.
A vase of roses on the upright piano —
it was dark mahogany, and the heavy
roll-top desk was oak —
a letter lying there unfinished,
interrupted when the family
arrived for Sunday tea.

The grandchildren are outside now,
the women in the kitchen still.
He'll sit a while then with his pipe
before returning to that letter —
legal matters — at once both dull

and painful — the complications
of his son's estate.

And while he sits and smokes
a sudden breath of wind
catches at the curtains,
sets the specks of light
dancing on the polished wood
and brings from the garden
with the smell of grass
the children's voices.

His mind slips then — time
folding over the wound —
and the sounds carried by the breeze
are the voices of his own children,
playing as they did in that
same garden thirty years before.

And so absorbed is he
in the re-emergence
of those other afternoons
that he fails to register the moment
when his own heart . . .
       . . . stops

Homecomings

No hearse, no tall black hats, no stiff attire
to greet Vangelis, shipped back to his island
from the mainland hospital. No sooner
is the stern door down than half a dozen
of his friends rush in and come out brandishing
elaborate floral banners, which they stack
against a bright red Mazda truck,
its tailgate lowered ready when four younger men
bring out, not shoulder-high but like a packing case,
the lace-trimmed casket which has travelled,
for convenience, in the car deck. It's loaded,
secured with a single loop of rope,
the banners laid each side, and old Vangelis
sets off on the last of many jolting rides
up to the village where the soil
that was his livelihood's prepared for him.

His widow, meanwhile, forgotten by the men
in their anxiety to get their friend ashore,
emerges unaccompanied from the hold
and takes a few uncertain steps.
But halfway down the ramp she stops and looks around.
A hand goes up to cover quivering lips
as she can gauge at last, against the blurring
outlines of this familiar waterfront,
the exact dimensions of her loss.

She won't be stranded there for long, between
the vessel that can carry her no further
and the shore she first set foot on as a bride,

before the women, waiting for this moment, will
envelop her, and, clutching both her arms,
will draw her back into their common life.

Greek mariners
or
The naming of craft

The heroes, gods and goddesses
have each their great steel funeral barge
that plies with living bodies, cars
and freight between the eroded fragments
of their former sun-loved haunts.

But saints, those heroines and heroes
of a less enlightened age,
with smaller, wooden craft, stay close
inshore, or, venturing out in shoals,
pursue pre-apostolic trade.

The secret beach

In other years they will be green again —
the banks along this road; the scars will heal;
the poppies and the swallowtails return;
       but raw my wound remain.

The old mule track was widened by machines.
They broke the rocks and broke the trees, but rains
of a single winter broke the road — deep trenches
       cut right through it by the streams.

The secret beach exposed and bare.
The carob trees that hedged it round are gone.
Their bones stick out among the stones — steep slopes
       of rubble that advance towards the sea.

Two years ago, when she was three, we came —
an hour's walk along the track from where we stayed —
and spent whole days here with the child;
       picked out among fine shingle

11

only the tiniest of shells.
Swam with her round a pointed rock, and hid
behind, then met again to kiss. A game.
      She called it "Visiting".

And I have visited again and almost
passed — unrecognized — this place, and sat
and held a smooth white pebble in my hand,
and watched the past recede — so fast — across
      the grey and troubled surface of the sea.

The bird, hatched from the stone I held, has flown.
But — its trajectory broken by the weight of memory —
it fell — a fragment of a childhood lost
beyond the reach where I would trust, as yet,
      my aching body to the waves.

A classical dichotomy
(Archaeological Museum, Thessaloniki)

So many marble heads without their bodies,
so many marble bodies without heads —
room after room — as though Time had been
quite willful in her carelessness.

Head or body? — Is that the choice she offers us?
Is it only in low relief we can hope to survive entire?

Coincidence
(1st of October 1991)

I picked up in the street today a bookmark.
A narrow strip of silk with tasselled ends.
Embroidered into it, in green, the word
DUBROVNIK.
                    I was there,
in nineteen-sixty-four or sixty-five,
for a few hours, or a day at most.
I remember only the greyish stone
and the vague outlines of old buildings,
the city walls . . . and a row of new
shop windows built into ancient stonework
(beautifully restored), displaying
. . . almost nothing.
                    Dubrovnik
comes back to me today, not only
from this lost or discarded souvenir
but also from the radio in the workplace
just minutes before I emerged
into the street and found it lying there:

> *The Croatian port of Dubrovnik*
> *has today been subjected*
> *to heavy shelling from the sea*
> *by the Yugoslav Federal Navy.*
> *Damage in certain parts of the city*
> *is said to be extensive.*

A royal dilemma
(Archaeological Museum, Thessaloniki)

Rarely in such places do the bones
have names already known to us, but these,
we're told, without a doubt are what remains
of Philip, King of Macedon and father
    to Alexander, called *the Great.*

Twenty-three centuries these bones,
inside a box of solid gold, itself
inside a marble chest, housed in a spacious
stone-built tomb, beneath a mound of earth,
    lay cramped and jumbled.

Now at least he can stretch out again —
now that his bits (some fixed with glue)
have been arranged in a more or less
    functional pattern.

But how exposed now in this perspex box
(poor substitute for gold) for anyone to peer at —
anyone who's passing through the city
with a thousand drachmas (free on Sundays)
    and an hour to spare.

Not, I think, what he'd have wanted
as a final fate; but rather to have stayed
forever in the stone tomb undisturbed
    behind the marble doors.

Poison on Poros

Whose is this unwashed marble face
stuck herm-like on a roughcast concrete post
that scowls at my approach? Ah, there's a name:
DEMOSTHENES. Hail, then, Demosthenes.
How are you, sir? And what are you doing at this
tarmac *trivium* on the edge of town?
Whoever set you up has left no clue.

Your resting place was in the hills behind,
within the *temenos* and in Poseidon's care.
You are the island's most illustrious suicide.
Or *were* — the Swedish archaeologists
may have removed you, unaware.

Dead friends

We meet
across a coffin,
with nothing but this
dead friend between us.

Your eyes
hard to meet,
and words to find —
fall apart in the space
between us
or slightly to the side,
where I confront
the tall red eyes
of your paraffin stove.

Your grief
still fresh, and mine
already exhausted
where in a dream
I left him
drifting, oarless
in a covered boat
along a narrow channel
underground.

After a while
my face-skin tightens
and I leave your house
not certain what it was
that words obscured.

— ◆ —

Years later
after many more
always rather
awkward meetings
— and once we tried,
together, with only
temporary success,
to persuade
another friend
to stay alive —
you too
must have decided,
alone, one night,
in that same room
where we first met
— and in the morning
the stove was still alight —
that it was better
never, ever
to remember
anything
again.

——— ◆ ———

Stephen Coates (d. 1969)

•

Harry Pincus (d. 1973)

•

Anni Soldi (d. 1974)

An old recording

"Well, Geoff, what d'you think of married life?"

It's summer nineteen-forty, their wedding
just a few weeks past, and she'll be thirty,
he'll be thirty-one. My uncle's just acquired
this new recording apparatus,
a machine for cutting discs,
and in a slightly formal, radio style
he interviews the happy pair.

"What d'you think of married life?" he asks.
And then you hear my father laugh,
as he sidesteps neatly from the question,
like the nifty dancer he was said to be.

"Ask me again," he says, "in ten years' time."

But the next recording — ten years
within a month or so — is cut in stone.
PEACE, it says, IN PROUD AND LOVING MEMORY . . .
and then his name and dates.

War dead

Rare the Greek village without its war memorial,
but few so elegant or eloquent as this, erected
by the village of Lemós for its "heroic sons,
fallen in the wars of nineteen-twelve to twenty-two".
A marble column with an olive branch in low relief;
on top a phoenix; and on the pedestal the names:
two on the front, killed in the Macedonian Struggle;
three on the left "lost without trace" in Asia Minor,
and on the right five more who "later died in hospitals".

About a half-day's march away, less elegant,
though no less eloquent, crudely outlined by a double,
crumbling concrete kerb, a single roadside grave,
once railed — three rusted posts with hooks remain —
a tiny marble cross, inscribed with one word — AGNOSTOS —
in a pass no doubt contested more than once, and home
to other bones than those of this poor solitary UNKNOWN.

In Salonica today the sea

Yesterday the sea was glittering, inviting,
at the end of every downhill street,
but today the sea, now that the wind has changed,
looks and smells like a drain.

Last night most of a moon was posing
in the branches of the trees above the park,
where, in the open theatre,
old Islamic poetry was declaimed
against the notes, solitary and aching,
or in nerve-bending clusters, plucked
from the tamboura.
                        Some Sultan,
were his love to remain unreturned,
would as well, he said, have been a slave
or camel driver. The moon, I suppose,
in the sixteenth — or the thirteenth — century,
looked much the same.
"Friend, aaaaah, friend," they cry.

In Salonica today the sea,
now that the wind has changed
looks and smells like the sewer that it is.
But the old men on *Leofóros Níkis*
are undeterred, their legs dangling
over the sea-wall, their baited hooks
below the brown scum.
Perhaps tonight on *Leofóros Níkis*
I shall pause, as yesterday, and watch
another sun smeared black with smoke

sucked down into the hills across the gulf.
Friend, aaaaah friend, perhaps tonight
on *Leofóros Níkis* you will tell me
whose that *Victory* might be.

At an Oxford conference

Thunder without rain; and voices —
some familiar — rising
from the courtyard to the window
of this monk-like attic room.
Voices distinct, but the words
blurred at the edges. And your body
a fading memory. Its absence
the outline of my solitude,
here, in this — in any — city.

This city, which you once knew without me,
I now learn without you. And,
though its streets indeed delight,
        delight lights less of me.

Thunder without rain; and clouds
roof in the courtyard, stifling the voices
rising to my window. The light fails
and the memory of your body fades —
        an unrestorable image.

Still life, Sigh . . . gone

The Ho Chi Minh City Museum now;
the Gia Long Palace in colonial times
and twenty years of post-colonial war.

It was there, in an upper gallery,
I met a water buffalo, and was
transfixed by its stare. Its head was turned a little
to the side, with one good eye and one bad.
Its backward-curving horns not fully grown.
Stuffed, and already looking rather threadbare.
A wadded rag and a brown rubber tube
protruding from its mouth suggested that
the taxidermist's job was not quite done.

But there was something in the way it stood
that seemed to say it was still young and eager;
frustrated, though, to find itself between
the shafts of a cart to which it wasn't hitched,
a heavy cart with solid wooden wheels
well worn, a long way now from being round.

It spoke to me, that buffalo, of lives
cut short, of lives unlived, of wasted years,
of all the time, men, money, armaments,
defoliants, stupidities and lies
it took America to get itself defeated here.

In the Commonwealth
Cemetery at Souda

Two, three hours in the heat
I walk between the rows of stones.
Methodically I pace each rank
in every ordered block
and read, obsessively,
each word on every stone —
all fifteen hundred of them — half-
expecting, in my sun-dazed trance,
to stumble on my father's name.

As likely I should find my own.
The army turned him down
on grounds of health, and he
was never out of England. Still,
some crazed derangement of my wits insists
I'll find him, not long married, dug-in here,
three years too soon for my conception.

Some names come close. But when I've read
them all what's left's the scattered few
who'd lost all trace of their identity.

At nearby Malemé each nameless German has
a brusque, straightforward UNBEKANNTE.
But here propriety, or piety, eschews such candour.
These Brits, Australians, New Zealanders
are KNOWN — like secret thoughts, or what
the future holds — ONLY TO GOD.

The last breakfast

On the morning of the day he died,
after Ralph, the night-nurse, had gone home,
my father, forty, months now in bed,
announced — so, years later, I was told —
that today he'd like a proper breakfast.
And though she knew he'd never eat it,
my mother went downstairs into the kitchen.

Fifteen minutes later, I would guess,
she came back carrying a tray
(bacon-and-eggs, buttered toast and coffee)
and found him standing, clutching the cill
of the window he'd pushed open wide,
leaning out in his striped pyjamas,
gasping for breath in the summer air.
She held him, and helped him back to bed,
covered him up and, once his breathing
settled, went downstairs again to phone;
came and sat with him, now barely conscious,
until she heard the doctor's car outside.

Sensing the condition of his patient
and deciding that the end was near,
he filled a syringe with morphine, sufficient
to ensure there'd be no more distress.

On the morning of the day *she* died,
my mother, twenty-six years later,
emerging briefly from her coma —
where, perhaps, wandering in the past,

she'd finally retrieved the husband
she'd never had the chance to mourn
and whose face, she had once said to me,
she couldn't remember any more,
and had at last mutely understood
her own condition — now announced,
having eaten nothing for a week,
that today she'd like a proper breakfast.

The effects of alcohol
In memory of David Cooper
(1931–1986), a sometime guest.

After you
we return to a bed
ravaged
by friendly arms
of occupation.

In the morning
begins again
the muted destruction
of the body.

In memoriam L.G.D.

Durrell, living in the hills of Cyprus
with an infant daughter, writes as Darley,
escaped with a few books and the child —
Melissa's child — to heal himself on some
unnamed Aegean island (snatched
each night from darkness by Arcturus)
where the Smyrna packet en route
from Alexandria's delayed
one Thursday night with engine trouble
and deposits on his doorstep Balthazar,
that fictional acquaintance of Cavafy
(the old poet of the city), clutching the manuscript
in which he has insinuated, interlinear,
one construct's perceptions, constructed to correct
another construct's reconstructions
of lives that no one ever lived,
the product of returning link by link
along the iron chains of memory
to a city inhabited so briefly . . .
Only the city — and its poet — wholly real.

Cavafy, dying, his voice already gone
and twenty-five poems still inside him,
on a clean sheet — his final act — inscribes
a circle, and at its centre marks a point . . .
How Lorca, living, longed to hear
the music of those Braque guitars!
And Darley, technically immortal,
will be here as always, writing by the water,
the night sky dusted thickly with stars.

Here's to you, Ma!

Seems a comfortless place to lie in —
this corner of the cemetery,
with the main Rochdale road
not twenty yards to your right,
and beyond your feet a broken wall
and the sagging ironwork
round what was once a tennis court —
you enjoyed a game, I bet
(about half a century ago) —
and then The Spotted Cow . . .

All these years and I've never once
had a pint in your local!

"No. Make that a double sherry, please."
That was more in your line.

. . . update on redevelopment
(February 2019)
with automotive digressions

By the time we laid you here to rest
the Cosy Nook cinema had gone
and, apart from the pub, the local
amenities were non-existent.

Later on, a BP filling station
sprang up across the road, but you'd

no need of petrol, oil or compressed air.
In your twenties, though, you'd owned a car,
when your work for the Women's League
of Health and Beauty took you,
and cousin Pamela, around the country.
And once, swerving to avoid a dog,
you drove your little Austin Seven
through a plate-glass window. The irate
owner of the shop said, understandably,
"You should've just run down the dog."

But in the ten years of your married life
you let your licence lapse. Then found yourself
a widow with a husband's car
you couldn't drive. The Morris Minor lived
in "Uncle" Ernie's garage down the road.
(He wasn't a real uncle but that's
the way we spoke of family friends.)
He and his blind wife had no use
for their garage and so housed our car
even when my father was still driving.
I was fascinated by the way
my blind "Auntie" moved about her kitchen
to make a pot of tea and set out
biscuits on a plate — amazed — in awe —
as though she was a being from
another planet, or perhaps
an eyeless angel who saw everything.
And — also strange — there was a stream —
elsewhere completely underground —
that ran through their suburban garden
with a pond they'd stocked with goldfish.

You used to say you'd take the Test again
but never quite got round to it.
Eventually the car was sold.

Some years ago The Spotted Cow
shut down for lack of customers.
Its yard became a home for Travellers.
The windows all got smashed, those
on the ground floor were boarded up.
The slates were taken from the roof.
You can still see it in this sorry state
(for a while at least) on Google Earth
if you've got Internet in Hades.

But now it's been demolished. The remnants
of the tennis court torn down as well.
But don't get too upset about all this,
for things are looking up! The area
will soon be livelier than ever
and you and your companions underground
won't lack for anything at all
with a brand-new branch of

L♦DL

on your doorstep.

. . . and twelve months later

Lidl has been delayed a bit, it seems,
but soon you'll have new neighbours,
now that the tennis court's become
a little group of small two-storey homes.

Anna Palaiologou's gate
(Thessaloniki)

Tonight I'm eating on the pavement, opposite
the Gate of Anna Palaiologou, plagued by cats,
mosquitoes and the smell — vaguely ecclesiastical —
from the uncorked phial on the plastic tablecloth
of slightly rancid olive oil. At the table
next to mine, three women of widely differing ages
are admiring jewellery the eldest one's just bought.
Bursting the bubble pack, she rips the earrings from the card
and clips them on. "They're lovely!" the other two exclaim.
The young one helps her fit around a wrinkled neck
a double string of ersatz pearls and black glass beads.

My food arrives. Its quality indifferent.

The widowed empress Anna Palaiologou stumped up
the cash for a new gateway in the city wall,
here where it meets the walls of the acropolis.
It seems some cheapskate builder got the job. The jambs
are not a pair, the lintel matches neither. Still,
she lends her name to an inscription on the left-hand
jamb (the one that's cracked right through)
in which she's honoured as "Our Lady and our Mistress
the Lady Anna Palaiologou".

A mourning walk on a spring afternoon
(Wednesday, 9 April 2014)

For nine months now the world has been without you;
my world for just two hours. And having wept
and given up working for the day, I walk,
to think of you, around the brave new world
of London's Docklands — territory unknown,
I think, to you — and think of Austrian
and German cities — all unknown to me —
where you had spent the last few years —
your last few years — and Klosterneuburg where,
last year in July, you died.

                   These last nine months
my world's been a deceit. I'd thought, at such
times as I thought of you at all, it was
a world that still contained you. We had, I know,
been out of touch a year or more. Three weeks
ago I'd something to communicate
to wildecat@ . . . and started with a joke
about your email name. But no reply.
And so today I searched the worldwide web
and found a Death Notice that had been printed
in a local paper: "Precious daughter . . .
and loving partner . . . tragic accident
at Klosterneuburg . . . sadly missed . . . At peace."

Was peace what the wildecat was looking for
on the bridge at Klosterneuburg from which she fell?

Beside the glittering Thames I think of you
amongst the wreckage that the tide's laid bare.

The lengths of rope, steel cables, both ends frayed,
cut off from everything they once had held.
The rotting pilings of long-vanished wharves.
And half a moon, pale silver-grey, face tilted up
into the soft blue sky. And muddy sherds
of corrugated sheeting that suggest
the ribs of broken boats. And briefly then
around my feet a peacock butterfly.
A Polish family on the river bank
with makeshift teepee and a driftwood fire.
They say they're homeless, have no money, but
"The sun is shining," and they smile, the boy
intent upon a box of bait and hooks.
Two fishing rods. "No fish today," they say.
The lap of water and a faint sea smell.
The great steam hammer from the blacksmith's shop
at Albert Dock stands in a park, immobile —
its own memorial — among the trees in bloom.

I stood, the seventeenth, in Burke's *Assembly*
of sixteen hollow iron men at Woolwich Arsenal;
now sit, a glass of bitter in my hands,
to contemplate a world in which you don't
exist. The evening light — the "golden hour" —
seems scarcely more than pale moon-grey tonight.

These things — the extravagant dark beauty of
the peacock above all — I offer you
in memory of your unlived years to come.

(A.J.D., d. 18 July 2013, aged 28)

Bashō, Oppenheimer, and a dream

I'd like to be proved wrong about what will come of
this atomic business. I was quite wrong in believing it
would cost us our freedom. Our lives are fairly good,
fairly peaceful. We seem to go untouched . . .
> (J. Robert Oppenheimer,
> the "father of the atomic bomb")

> Determined to fall
> a weather-exposed skeleton
> I cannot help the sore wind
> blowing through my heart.
> (Bashō)

So here I am in the middle way, having had twenty years —
Twenty years largely wasted, the years of *l'entre deux guerres*
Trying to learn to use words . . .
> (T. S. Eliot)

The beginning lost in silence
the end drowned out by noise
at points too remote to distinguish
the real from the imagined.

I come to this word-making late
having had fifty *years* —
and more — *largely wasted,*
the years of l'après *deux guerres*
and the third always impending.

The lost time weighs on me as though,
with the roof of the inner chamber fallen in,
the hundreds of tons of soil in a burial mound

pressed down upon the corpse, and especially now,
at twilight, when, on an empty stomach,
a single glass of wine has opened doors
behind my eyes and my mind lies unshielded
from the glare of the day's cremation
where colours deepen as the light dies.

Late evening after sun-scorched August day
and dark now. Chill in the air, and stars.
Faint moon shadows from the trees
shift about uneasily
among the coarse grass and thistles
of this neglected orchard.

— ◆ —

Once he called it "sweet",
that thing he'd had a hand in making
in the forties at Los Alamos,
New Mexico, speaking, I suppose,
purely as a physicist — theoretically —
sensing its formal perfection,
feeling as Bach might have felt
emerging from that narrowness of vision
the creative act — after the first flush —
requires, the notes still wet,
the last bars of *Matthäus Passion*
soundlessly ringing in his ears.

— ◆ —

34

But even at the dress rehearsal
our physicist–conductor entered
in the ledger of congratulations
a discordant note. "I am," he said,
quoting some loose translation of the *Gita* —
his own perhaps (he'd learned some Sanskrit) —
"I am become death, the shatterer of worlds",
as he watched the fruiting body form
and spread its stain across the desert sky
above "Point Zero", which he himself
had christened "Trinity", after
the destructive yet renewing *force*
to break, blow, burn of Donne's *three person'd God.*

The military of course held all performing rights
and promptly fixed the date and venue for the world première,
with repeat performance from a slightly altered score
provisionally scheduled, in case demand should warrant it,
a few days later in another place.

Hiroshima. Nagasaki. Twin stars of our birth.
There were the last Greek statues shattered. *There*
the oldest of the gods arose, and, taking
to themselves, adding to their list of thousands,
two new names, "Fat Man" and "Little Boy",
they laughed, seeing no longer hidden
what they had always known, that we,
not they, are figments of imagination.

Escaped at last into what's left
of light and air and time, stumbling up
an endless-seeming spiral stair
from the bright-lit schoolroom, where,
two/three hundred feet below the ground,
seated at neat rows of desks
under neon tubes and listening to
the generator's comfortable hum,
the soft swish of air conditioning,
we'd watched on flickering screens in black and white
the all-but-final stages of our play —
the great cloud rising, *little as a human hand*,
the blinding light made "viewable".

Escaped from "shelter" underground
and staggering towards the river bed
through mud and debris, among broken sheds —
some vast and long disused industrial estate —
and at our backs the half-obliterated sky.

Escaped into what's left
of light and air and time
to entertain our deaths together
crouched on this bank beside
the wooden-boarded iron bridge
that spans a dried-out river.
And ghosts go past, ghosts
of Hiroshima, ghosts
of Nagasaki, those
known before only
as a stain on a pavement
or a shadow on a wall,

who, having now retrieved
their bodies from the air,
dance across the bridge
in borrowed clothes — old men
with tambourines and bells,
their wood-soled sandals clattering,
the sleeves of gold-embroidered
black kimonos flapping, shouting,
singing as they move towards
the objects of our dread.

And when they've passed, we crawl
across the bridge the other way,
emerging upright in a tree-lined
wide suburban street. Leaf and light
of summer afternoon. Absurd familiarity
of pillar box. And an old man with a beret
glides slowly past us on a bicycle.

Years later, after he'd been investigated
and returned to teaching, or maybe even later,
when too ill for that — and this perhaps
was never written down, but simply
something *Oppie* said to Bateson
in the course of private conversation —

"The world" he said "is moving towards Hell"
(*I am become death, the shatterer of worlds*)
"with a high velocity" (speaking as a physicist)
"and a high acceleration and"
(most definitely here the physicist)

"a high rate of change of acceleration."

"And perhaps" he continued (now the Quietist)
"the only chance there is that it won't get there"
(and here the syntax gets a little strange,
though I remember it, I think, as Bateson gave it,
speaking in London in the sixties)
"the only chance there is that it won't get there
is if we are willing to let it."

— ◆ —

And Bashō

        the beginning lost in silence

determined to fall

        the end drowned out by noise

a weather-exposed skeleton,

how could he help

        at points too remote to distinguish

the sore wind

        the real from the imagined

blowing through his heart?

———— ◆ ————

Memorials
(1941, 1989)

"The German monument," the *Blue Guide Crete*
asserts with evident distaste, "takes
the aggressive form of a diving eagle."
But that eagle was their badge,
those *Fallschirmjägern, hunters* from the sky.

THIS MEMORIAL
    caught up now in the town's westward sprawl
WAS ERECTED NINETEEN-FORTY-ONE
    when it would have stood alone
    on a bare slope against the sea
BY GERMAN PARACHUTISTS
    and the inscription — at the base
        of the long wide flight of granite steps
        that rises between a house
            with goats and chickens in the yard
            an old woman and three small children
            eating at an outside table
        and a building plot cut back
            at road level deep into the hill
            and ready for another house
            a restaurant or a petrol station
        towards the solid tower
        of square-cut yellow stone that holds
        the gigantic eagle frozen in its fall —
    the inscription is in German
    and in English and in Greek
FOR THEIR DEAD COMRADES.

The Greek has, not FOR, but TO THE MEMORY OF
THEIR, not DEAD, but FALLEN COMRADES
tom besóndon symbolemistón don
to whom the drumbeat of those plural genitives
seems to pay an ungrudged tribute.
And the Greek noun more precise
with a force that our *comrades* has lost
(and *comrades-in-arms* sounds too genial)
for the Greek comrades, the *symbolemistés,*
are *those who make war together* —
which would seem to encompass the enemy.

Does that explain — taken
with the pride the Cretan people felt
in the slaughter of so many
of those invaders from the sky
    some shot like birds and dead
       before they hit the ground
    and some who fell screaming
       into the clutch of old men waving swords
       whose rusty blades recalled
       the last revolts against the Turks,
       of women armed with farm tools,
       children with sticks and stones
       and even dogs come out to welcome
       these "liberators" as their briefing
       had assured them they would be —
does that explain why this monument still stands
when Cretan anger pulled down so much else in forty-five?

    Only the "twisted cross" as it's called in Greek

was stripped from the block of stone
still gripped between the eagle's claws.

— ◆ —

Later, on a narrower road, I find
another, accidental and perhaps more fitting
memorial to those fallen *Fallschirmjägern.*

Level with my eyes, six feet away,
on its back, wings spread, impaled, where,
shot out of the sky, it had fallen —
strange fruit in the crown of a thorn that grew
from the steep bank below the road —
a crow looked at me with one eye — defiant . . .
    . . . *all ye that pass by* . . .

———— ◆ ————

Ka and Kavafis

For Ioulia
in whose house it came to me
and in whose old notebook
the first drafts were written.

Minutes before it reached him
the poet Ka
in Pamuk's novel *Snow*
could feel a poem coming.

And he'd stop
what he was doing —
in social situations
he'd retreat into a corner,

caught in the street
make for the nearest teahouse,
get out his notebook
and have it open, ready.

Cavafy
recalling a visitor
he'd just received — a young poet
without means, unemployed,

thus always there,
a faithful servant to his Art —
bemoaned the many times
a fine idea

or some rare image
had come to him at work;
lines unexpected, ready-made
been set aside

because some office task was pressing
and then at home
he'd try to call them back
and find they'd gone.

He'd told the poet
how dearly he had paid
for the little luxuries
his salary allowed.

Eighteen of the nineteen poems Ka wrote
in four enchanted days
in Kars were lost
the night he died.

One was preserved — mostly audible —
on videotape in Kars
but for the rest
just summaries,

titles, brief quotations
in the copious notes Ka made
those last four years in Frankfurt
after Kars.

The night that Ka was shot
between the station
and his Frankfurt flat
he'd just returned from Hamburg

where he'd been reading
to a Turkish audience from —
as witnesses confirmed —
the green Kars notebook,

which must have been taken,
the evidence suggests,
by his — still unidentified —
assailant.

Cavafy's *Unfinished Poems* —
lacking, it may be,
those very lines
his luxuries had cost him —

survived his death
and (still unfinished)
did eventually
(six decades later) reach his readers.

What we, Ka's would-be readers, need
to satisfy
our curiosity
is some new fiction,

in which the lost green notebook
comes to light
with all the incomparable poems
Ka wrote in Kars.

Then Ka, we know, will take his place
beside Zhivago
among the greatest poets
who never lived.

The family plot,
Salendine Nook Baptist Cemetery
(with a moderate Yorkshire accent)

Just past the old bus terminus
with its turning circle for the trolleys
before they set off back to town
(they're all diesels now the buses)
there's the Baptist Chapel
with its plain black walls.
There were spaces still
to be had there in the graveyard
long after Saint Stephen's was full up.
And so, though nominally C of E,
it's there they lie . . . and rot,
my mother, father, his father and his mother too
but not for her the rot, somewhat
refined by fire she was
for she'd a horror of waking in a coffin —
had read too much that kind of stuff
("I like a good murder," she would say
if you noticed her bedside reading) —
and had the doctor promise, years before,
he'd slit the arteries in her wrists "just to be sure"
before he signed the death certificate.

Of course he didn't do it, promise or no,
but she'd've forgotten too by then,
dying slowly, bit by bit,
her body being the last to go.

They died in the wrong order anyway.

No! — not the bits of her, the four of them.
He was the first, my father, "struck down
in the prime of life," as people said.
I was only five, I didn't go
to the funeral, I didn't know,
they didn't tell me
until after they had buried him
that he was dead.

Ten when my grampa went.
Away at school. They didn't think
to fetch me back. "Not suitable for children,"
they'd've said. Big funeral too.
He'd been well known in town and the police
turned out in force. No, not that! —
he'd been a top-rank Special Constable
and knew them all. The football people
and the lawyers came as well. "Hundreds
and hundreds lined the streets," the paper said
(my mother kept the cutting).

My grandmother's cremation
was a quiet affair — I was grown up then —
and we left it to the undertaker's men
to deposit, at a later date,
her ashes in the grave, and so
I never saw it opened up until
my mother died some ten years later
(I had two children of my own by then).

There was some doubt
on that occasion, about

how deep they'd dug it to begin with
and the undertaker — we knew him well,
his firm did joinery too
and he'd had an elegant little
walnut table of my mother's,
one of a nest of tables, wedding present,
in his shop for years,
supposed to mend it but he never did
and in the end she'd got fed up
and fetched it back herself, carried it
home on foot and glued it up
as best she could. Held up alright
even though it didn't look so good —
so the undertaker, as I was saying,
wasn't sure that she would fit
and said he'd have to go
and check the records in the book.

When he popped back next day
the family were assembled in the lounge,
there were visitors as well, the room
was full and several people had to stand.
I didn't see him right away
stood just inside the door with hat in hand
holding it as if it were a fig leaf.
And when he finally caught my eye
he craned his neck and raised his brows
giving me a confidential kind of look:

"Room for two at Salendine Nook," he said.

Well, there was only our mother ready at the time

and so that still leaves room for one
but whether for my sister or for me
we've not discussed and I suppose
that we'll just have to wait and see
which one of us is first to catch the bus.

Nightscapes,
   seascapes,
   lovescapes,
      landscapes . . .

Night conceits

You turn away to seek your other lover — Sleep,
who thee in thine own arms doth now enfold,
who takes you, so sudden always and so strong,
and holds you to him, tight and close,
      all hours of the night.

And me you leave to contemplate
the symptoms of desire, and all those small
brown marks, scattered like stars across the pale
      expanses of your back.

Some faint, as in the starwash of the Milky Way.
Others, the major constellations, dark and clear.
Your back — a universe as closed to me
      as are your eyes, your arms.

Condemned by the obstinate throb of lust to wake,
I sit up now beside you in the bed.
You stir and turn towards me blind — rapt, still,
      in his embrace.

O'er that broad river that betwixt us runs
your breath comes hard and deep, rippling like reeds
the soft hairs on the margins of my arm
and forming on the steep bank of my thigh
      a small cold place.

Night out on Thasos

The noisy flapping of the last few crows,
come back to sit the night out in their trees.
Nine hours of dark ahead of us — the crows and me.

A thousand metres now above the sea,
from which I set out in the midday August heat,
hoping for cooler nights up here among the pines.

The flies have gone, and slowly, one by one at first,
the stars hatch out. They smell of resin and they sound
like crickets in the brittle grass.

Attic power cut
ὦ γαῖα καὶ νὺξ ἣν ἐδερκόμην πάρος

Tonight, reading *Electra*
fails to electrify. The book
slips and I fall asleep
before slaughter can dispel
the "dark" she's "clearly seen",
and wake — the candle still burning —
bathed in a cool green light,
as the motions of the spheres effect
the periodic, brief alignment
of my face, the skylight, and the moon.

Lunch on Poros

This winter-lunchtime seafront restaurant
makes few concessions to modernity.
A glass-front fridge with meat, and some soft drinks.
A structure of steel I-beams (four by twos),
carrying above a row of wooden tables
four huge oak barrels filled with local wine.

The plaster's painted white; wood panelling
and barrel ends a bleached Hellenic blue.
Lace curtains cover windowless recesses.
Prints of ships have wrinkled in their frames.
The chicken's roasted to destruction, but
the rest — the fried potatoes, salad, cheese —
perfection; and the kindly wine will soften,
for a while, the day's metallic edge.

Saturday night
and Sunday morning

What is a life when you lie in the dark
between reading and sleeping,
take out your heart
and feel in your hand
its uncertain beating,
and the tall hibiscus is outlined
against faint streetlight
filtered through the blind,
and the one beside you sleeps so easily.

What is a life when you wake in the light
on a Sunday, late,
and see between the slats
before your mind's in place
the aerials scratched —
black lines on grey across the sky,
and the one beside you reads a book,
and a single church bell tolls
its invitation to another world.

"I do not think that they will sing to me"

I saw her standing in the doorway opposite.
Dark skin, black hair, and wearing only white —
a short tight skirt, close-fitting fine-knit
V-necked sweater, shaped so perfectly
by her firm breasts, her narrow waist.

Young, but not so very young, say twenty-six.
Smiling, relaxed, and talking to a painter,
who was also black and also wearing white —
his painter's overalls and cap —
and lounged against the gate and laughed.

As I left the house to go and buy some bread
I saw her standing in the doorway opposite
and I was trapped in mine. My eyes were stung by beauty
and my heart was dragged across the street to join
this vision of an easier, more immediate life.

I saw her standing in the door across the street
and though I tore my eyes away at last, her shape came too
and overlays whatever else I see and taunts me
with the limits of my circumstance, with being
middle-aged and middle-class and overweight and white.

Should I, then, being white, wear black —
now I have seen this vision of my unlived life,
have seen her standing in the door across the street —
wear always black like Chekhov's Masha,
who dragged her life behind her like an endless train.

Or should I, like Masha, shake myself
and throw it off? Should I, as Masha would have done,
root out this love and tear it from my heart?
When Masha married there would be no time for love.
And Masha was in mourning for her life.

Hearing the dawn

Birdsong and raucous laughter.
Not that that woke me. Awake
before the first bird. Before
they came back drunk next door,
flung doors and windows open
on the garden, exchanging
crude banter, oblivious
of the blackbird, he of them.
Broadcast on different frequencies.

Alone and silent, I am tuned to both.
And, with the day just edging
black flowers on the curtains into bloom,
give up all thought of sleeping.

Dawn ferry

Tired from a night flight, and ill, unable
to speak above a throaty whisper,
you sleep, slumped across me. My right arm,
resting on the table, pillows your head —
its disordered mass of curls and those
tortoise-shell combs you keep losing.
My left arm curls round you, your shoulder's
lodged against my chest, your hand
lying lifeless in my lap. The several
soft pressures of your body conduct
the throbbing of the engines to my groin
and when the boat docks and I wake you
I'm in no fit state to stand up.

Riding at anchor

Moored side by side on the beach,
limbs lashed together, our bodies
move in unison, buoyed
on the rise and fall of our breathing,
as though the sand swayed gently beneath us
in time to the waves idly breaking,
a yard beyond our feet.

Aegean snapshots 7 x 5

For Rose, who said the sea was silk and fell asleep.

Light from water
on the bows of resting boats
forms flickering nets in which
all too willingly
the mind is caught.

— ◆ —

A bitch straining at the leash, she scents the open sea
but her starboard anchor's badly snagged and drags her nose
round from the harbour mouth. She struggles and breaks free,
her engines leap, she vents her pent-up rage in two
great bursts of black smoke from her funnels, and is gone.

— ◆ —

In the harbour's clear green water, fish, neatly segregated
into groups by shape and size, pursue, at different depths,
their predetermined diets, like Orthodox and Muslims
in their adjacent, separate villages in Thrace —
potential catches for the statesmen's graded nets.

— ◆ —

Breaking the surface
of the antique
(Socratic) frog-pond,
a dolphin disperses
remnants of our plastic art.

— ◆ —

An isolated patch of cloud,
a pirate copy of the map of Crete,
has drifted northward, increasingly
contorted with dry laughter as it
hovers between Thrace and Samothrace.

Twice the stars it takes to plough the sky
have dropped onto the sea tonight
and in the last flaring of their dying fire
(tinged yellow by the brine) have formed
the waning constellation of the Fishing Fleet.

Scarcely ruffled in the August dawn
the indigo-blue velvet of the sea
is trimmed with white lace where it touches
ageing *Arsinoe*'s painted hull —
Aegean dress for an Egyptian queen.

When I arrived, one day years ago

Was it weeks or months since I had seen you
now that we lived so far apart in different towns?
Your room so welcoming when I arrived —
all those familiar objects — familiar from other
rooms and years — inextricably a part
of the YOU I carried in my mind.

The rush matting on the floor,
your old grey oil stove with its tall chimney,
big belly, bent legs and blue flames (sometimes)
in its eyes; the browns and yellow ochres
of your cooking pots and bowls.

There was someone coming out the house
as I arrived. They let me in, and, coming upstairs
quietly, I surprised you, playing your guitar, with books
spread all around you on the faded red
and brown and orange stripes of Indian cotton
that always lay across your bed.

You didn't move when I came in, stayed sitting,
plucking at the strings, twisting your song
into a greeting, while I picked out a wooden bowl
and filled it with the cherries I had brought
and set it down beside you
                                        and suddenly my hands
are filled with your breasts, the cherries slightly bitter
as our wet lips meet. The books we scatter
to the floor, throw off the covers from the bed,
fighting to possess each other's clothes —

in such a hurry that it takes an age,
but breathless with laughter and desire we collapse
at last together on the bed. I hold you
and I hold, it seems, all world I'll ever know
or want, but time can't stop, the urgency of lust
must drive us on and pleasure mount
towards its breaking point . . .

Dying and dying, shall we be born as huge flowers?
Where you breasts rub against me rivers flow.
My mind is washed away and I am carried by the flood
far out, and off the world's edge

fall . . .

. . . land softly

(is it hours later?) on white sheets beside you, the orange
glow of a summer evening, and you smile "Hallo".

Waking from dreams

Wake
in a hot and strangely patterned room
    and have to make
an effort to remember why you're here.

Walk
across thickly padded carpet to the door
    and talk
to yourself to tease out tangled strands of fear,
residual from unremembered dreams.

— ◆ —

Waking, midday, on a river bank,
blinded by sun, and muttering already
in my sleep familiar words,
felt for a moment that I understood
what game it was life played with me,
but a cloud crossed and the notion vanished,
scuttled though the reeds and plopped
into the water like a startled rat,
leaving only a faint wisp of sound drifting
in the air, an image blurred and shifting
    as a dream lost.

— ◆ —

Dream after dream
    lost
down the plughole of awakened eyes.
And the walls of the room
more faint each dawn,

worn
by the fine abrasion of revolving light.

Ropes
fray towards breaking on their mooring points
but the little ship contains
no expectation of the coming drift
unfettered on a widening sea
where no days dawn
to punctuate the night.

———— ◆ ————

Volcano days

The surface of the earth is hard and cold
but at its core the rock still boils — so you!
And I have known you in your rare volcano days,
gone down a willing victim to the onrush
of your lust; and you have ridden over me —
solitary Horseman of my Apocalypse,
my Whore of Babylon, bejewelled, glowing, wearing
Aphrodite's blind and blood-soaked smile.

I have known you in your rare volcano days;
and lost you in the awful, ordinary
silence after, when the ash, settling,
mixes with the household dust
and, eyes averted, we resume our roles,
ant-like creatures in the plains below.

Visitors

At India's breezy southern tip
where two seas and an ocean meet:
Kanniyakumari, Cape Comorin.
Two small rock islands lie nearby.
One's a philosopher's memorial
with meditation hall that brings
great hordes of pilgrims to the town.
On the other stands a Tamil poet.
He's almost thirty metres tall
and over forty with his plinth.
He's gazing back towards the shore
where now a group of women, young
and not so young, strung out in line,
are playing in the shallows — laughing,
shouting, splashing one another,
their saris soaked in brine — at least
it stops them billowing in the wind.

A wing-free squadron of multicoloured angels
on leave from sombre and celestial duties,
bearing no news, delivering no warnings,
just taking a brief holiday on earth
to taste the simple pleasures of the mortals.

From the Manickam Tourist Home
(Kanniyakumari, Tamil Nadu, India)

The view from the northside balconies
(admittedly the back) of this almost
smart hotel is not perhaps exactly
what the Western visitor expects —
an old, vast and long disused, partly filled-in
ritual bathing tank (it would have been empty
now but for the recent and unseasonal
heavy rains — the monsoon's early warning),
the verges strewn with hotel waste, scavenged
by dogs, cats, crows and a large troop of pigs
in which every size from two tiny piglets
to a great old boar is represented.
One man sits on the steps washing his feet.
Another crosses the filled-in grassy part,
crouches at the water's edge to wash
his arse, dries his left hand on his dhoti.

Looking out again next day at dawn
on a much more peaceful scene — one solitary
man, bathed in the orange glow, is facing me
across the water, his dhoti open
and his left hand on his penis, calmly
and slowly masturbating, as though
it were some sacred morning ritual
to induce a meditative trance.

Air India to JFK

The big blue Atlantic
pock-marked with white.
Obscured again now
by drought-cracked fields of cloud.

Reading Jane Austen
(*Mansfield Park*),
higher than the Himalayas
I eat an Indian meal.

Then it's films or sleep.
Obliged by gestures
from the man in front
reluctantly I close my blind.

Celestial multiplex —
same film on every screen,
half the stalls asleep now —
sweeps blindly on.

Princeton porches

Princeton's a lovely place
with too many inhabitants
too much concerned with wallpapers,
the latest coffee flavours,
and medical insurance.

In the affluent areas
it's amazing how many
houses have one or two
shiny white rocking chairs
on the front porch that look
for all the world as though
they never have been rocked in.

In the Hispanic neighbourhood
the people really do
sit out on their front porches
in rocking chairs, or maybe
on the porch steps, or just
on ordinary chairs with legs,
talking and laughing, smoking
and drinking beer from bottles.

It's almost as dark now
as it gets, and I'm walking
slowly back towards my lodgings
on the very edge of town
up Jefferson, and failing
to imagine myself living
in one of these detached

and splendid wooden houses
nestling among the trees.

Cloudscapes

Peering down midflight through scattered cloud,
perpelexed at first by all those
rugged, unfamiliar islands
in the Sea of Crete . . . Ah! Yes. — Cloud shadows
on the wind-carved surface of the sea.

With the lower slopes enveloped
in a dense, blue haze, the snow-capped
summit of Mount Ida floats
serenely past us through the sky.

It's early morning, and a dog
is barking at the waves; the wind
harries the sea; and a whole
new range of mountains
has arrived in the night.
Cold and grey and barren,
they tower above the upper village,
dwarfing yesterday's pale hills.
And I'm afraid that it will take
more than the wind to shift them now.

Monastic silences in Kefalonia

The dog had barked at my arrival, but the sign
PLEASE CLOSE THE GATE had seemed invitation enough,
and the dog had soon lost interest (the afternoon
was very hot) and had retreated to the shade.

I'd called out "Good day" when the old monk emerged
from his cell, carrying a coffee pot and cup,
but he hadn't acknowledged my greeting. The dog
got up and stretched and yawned and shook itself and went
to join him on the concrete bench against the wall.

He spoke to it from time to time and patted it
and sipped his coffee noisily and smoked a cigarette
and coughed and spat, and once or twice he did just glance
in my direction, in the half-hour that we sat there
no more than twenty yards apart, with just a walnut
and a lemon tree and — if we discount the coffee
and the cigarette — about a thousand years between us.

Feeling rested — it had been a long climb
up to the monastery — I walked across to where he sat.
"Are you alone here ?" I asked. He just looked at me,
indifferent, I think, not hostile, perhaps a bit
contemptuous. "It's peaceful here," I tried again.
Another silence. Then he spoke — a single word:
"German?" "No," I said, "English," and left it that,
but went on staring, rather longer I suppose
than was polite, into those dark eyes, set like knot-holes
in a face no less gnarled than the roots of this olive
where I'm sprawled now outside the gate and notice suddenly

the bells from the ruined campanile — earthquake
of nineteen-fifty-three — hung on chains about chest-high
from a rusted steel I-beam slung between two trees.

Hangovers

Inside my head three pairs of feet
are treading grapes. I wonder
whose they are, those feet,
and when the wine will be ready.

— ◆ —

Someone is stroking my head
with a cricket bat. Or is it a hand?
Or a dead cat, casually strolling
a high wall, skilfully avoiding
the strategic broken glass
to cut the hands and feet
of climbers-in or climbers-out
of this dark garden where nothing
grows and birds don't sing?

The railway station in Kampala

So this is the station where we'd planned to arrive.

Consulting first our old *Times Atlas of the World* —
separate pages for North and Central Africa —
we'd traced with fingers the black lines of railway tracks,
and, finding that the line from Egypt going south —
that was our grand idea — stopped short in the Sudan,
we'd had to accept Mombassa as our starting point.

We'd take the clear black line northwest then west
along the northern shore of Lake Victoria
to Kampala and beyond, and on the way we'd
get a taste of Africa's varied landscapes. But,
as we soon discovered, between Nairobi
and Kampala, all passenger services
had been suspended some four years before, and had,
in any case, been Tuesdays only . . . overnight.

So this is the station where we'd hoped to arrive.
The façade is neatly rendered, the render grooved
and coloured to suggest fine-jointed sandstone blocks.
No station name, but white on green in cursive script
Rift Valley Railways on the concrete canopy
that shades the entrance. Folding metal grilles are drawn
across and chained and locked. But through them can be seen
the clean-swept booking hall with gallery above,
two red machines of once-familiar English type
for PLATFORM TICKETS, and the tracks beyond. Next door
Headquarters of the Uganda Railways Corporation,

73

whose signboard still advises us BE SURE – GO RAIL.

The station clock, more honest and more up to date,
has all its numbers, but no hour or minute hand.

An Antique Valentine

Do'st harbour still within thine heart
(tho' no wound shews) that dart
whereon my name was writ, that Cupid shot?
How is it then thou lov'st me not?
Or did his arrow merely pass thee by,
grazing but the skin, and passing catch thine eye
for one brief moment? — Brief and yet
'twas long enough for that thou did'st forget
thou had'st resolv'd to keep thine heart thine own.

'Twere better had he altogether miss'd the mark
and never in thy breast Love's wild hope sown,
which, long unwater'd and confinèd in the dark
of thy deep-hidden soul, yields not to thee
that blood-red flow'r of joy thou should'st've had of me.

Speculum, speculum
or
In my Lady's Chamber

These, at sagging end and chapter's close,
standing humbly before the tables spread,
in the apsidal houses, who intend life:
   between the sterile ornaments
  under the pasteboard baldechins . . .
David Jones, *The anathemata*, "Rite and foretime"

The aging of my body and my face
is a wound from a terrible knife.
   C. P. Cavafy, "The melancholy of Jason
   Cleander, poet in Commagene, 595 AD"

In the Lady Chapel at Ely
there's a large rectangular mirror
mounted, like a table top
(but higher and tilted slightly),
on an oversize tea-trolley
to be wheeled about along
the central aisle of grave-slabs,
offering effortless inspection
of the gaudily re-coloured
bosses in the fan-vault ceiling —
clumps of foliage, angels, demons,
single roses and the bust
of a buxom wench (with swain),
the Green Man and the Crucified;
the centre boss, a couple, naked:
our first progenitors (with tree) —
or else a handy, tempting pool

75

for the unwary Narcissus,
aging, myopic and stiff-necked.
For such as him, or me,
that trolley really needs
a mental-health warning:
    NOT SUITABLE FOR USE
    BY PERSONS OVER FORTY.

If you've never bent to peer
into a horizontal mirror
since your facial muscles first
began to lose their tone,
    THEN DON'T.
It really can't be recommended.

My first though was "My God!
That's how I appear to any Lady
lying under me in love"
(or words to that effect).

Despite a life-long
interest in churches
the missionary position's
never been my favourite.
But since this Ely revelation
I've been even more determined
to ensure my nose remains
firmly pointed at the ceiling;
and it takes considerable
persuasion — or some
experience in martial arts
(a black belt helps)

to get me on my knees,
unless of course the sun's
already sunk, the lights
not lit, my Lady's Chapel
    CLOSED.

Little deaths

A spasm — long and shuddering —
but I wake dry, spilling seed only
on the white sheets of my dream.
There too I was alone —
no pale arms conjured to embrace me
nor soft breasts press against me
nor supple limbs entwine
nor burning fingers guide
the concentrated point of my desire
to the dark cave where annihi-
lation and ecstasy consort,
into the slaughterhouse of love
where the slain are reborn and return
      again and again.

Bodily comfort

I sensed she was there and reached out behind,
took the weight of a breast in my hand.
(Strange manoeuvre
but such things come easy in dreams.)

She stepped back a moment, uncovered both breasts
and held them towards me — I saw without seeing,
then turned and felt again against my outstretched palms
nipples rise and harden.

Such voiceless and unlooked-for reassurance
from that half-known being of the night-world
reaches out now to soften
the bitterness of this grey April day.

Lilies of the valley

Murder dead loves' ghosts;
take off shoes at dawn;
wander slowly
through the early shadows of your breasts.

Fingers moving over paper
retrace the contours
of your eyes;
feet rediscover cold stone.

Lips soften
the wrinkled organs of memory;
flowers open,
stretch towards their natural death.

Can hands that so easily met
move without tearing the skin
or paper walls
hold back the flames?

The sun which lay so long
beneath us in the dark
now has traced
its antique circle round our eyes.

Dawn finds me quiet
in front of these tiny white flowers
drying and dying
in a wineglass.

For a daughter born
12.45 a.m.
(6 February 1969)

I saw you born
    in blood and water
watched your wrinkled skin
    fill out
and your veins
    turn red.

I heard your cries
    and watched you blink
and thought of a woman
    waking
from long sleep
    to bright dawn.

I saw your dark eyes
    searching
but couldn't tell
    if you saw me
in a green gown
    and a white paper hat
with a mask
    where a mouth
should have been.

I must apologize
    for my appearance
at our first meeting,
    Isabel,

and tell you
   that my heart
wore gold and brown for you,
   sang mad and tearful
midday-sunlight-thunder-songs
   to celebrate
the midnight
   of your cruel freedom.

Remember me to him

Five pairs of eyes inform the room.
Tentative voices seek attentive ears.
But the voice of the child speaks loud —
unhindered gestures of sound
from his world of no-names
to which words have forgotten us.

Long ago

"Grandma is dead. So we all
move up a generation
and now the children are missing."

. . . and two generations later

Now, with the birth of a granddaughter,
the thread of life seems to have slipped
from my hands, my son taking my place.

Nothing has changed, though. I remain
where I always was; but lighter, much lighter
when I hold her sleeping in my arms.

This tenuous connection
with one who cannot speak,
this tiny wordless human, safe
for a while in her un-knowing —
a soothing ignorance, in which,
for these few moments, I can share.

Mouse poem for a child

There was a mouse who had no tale
to tell, or sell, who couldn't spell
the simplest words like "and" and "if",
whose head was empty — only sunlight
and the thoughts that flow as clear as streams
and mouselike dreams of infinite cheese.
No thoughts of "thems", no thoughts of "wes",
or cats, or rats whose greater strength
a mouse would go to any length
to keep from background of his mind.
He stands with solid wall behind
as sunlight warms his store of rind
and has no thoughts of any kind.
This is the mouse who has no tale
and as the evening sun turns pale
he turns to dreams, and though he seems
content, no words can tell if all is well
within the curtained mouselike world.

Minoan royal prerogative

Returning with his fellows from a morning's sport,
where the road rises, steep, towards the palace,
at the point where the cobbles begin,
he noticed, overturned among the stones,
a large brown beetle, its legs churning the air.
He bent down, put the nail of his right forefinger
under the beetle's back, and slowly turned it over.
He sat back, squatting on his heels, and waited
until the beetle reached the safety of the grass.

His companions would have laughed out loud,
had he not been their prince, at this man who,
not an hour before, surprising a frightened hare
amongst the scrub, had taken and killed it with his hands.

Autumn in Chania

Then suddenly it was cold
and the sea came over the harbour,
ran up the narrow alleys
unloading its cargo of seaweed
among the café tables, insisting
that the season was finished.

And overnight the pace of the city
changed. No more standing about now
except in the steamy bars.
No evening stroll, but hurrying
through the streets with hunched shoulders,
bent forward into the wind
and frowning, with coats and scarves
and lives pulled tight around us.

Tomb of Antipatros,
a Macedonian

The sort of gravestone that might well
have prompted something from Cavafy.
The date is suitable, third century
A.D., as is his age at death —
just twenty five. As for the rest
we learn only his father's and
his mother's names, his Rymitalkis,
hers Ammia, and that their son
      had died a hero.

But can we make of this young man
depicted, as conventional for heroes,
on a horse, approaching a seated,
shrouded figure, accompanied by a dog,
one of the "valiants of pleasure"?

More promising it seems to me,
though almost totally effaced
and scarcely visible behind
the horse's proudly lifted tail,
a young attendant, his back against
the left-hand edge of the relief,
who could, conceivably, have loved
this, perhaps too high-minded, hero
with a love that might well not
in any case have been returned.

An die ferne Geliebte

Emerged from cramped and fitful sleep,
peer through an oval of scratched perspex
at a premature Atlantic dawn.
A stranger seated among strangers
and unfamiliar even to myself
now that your image is taking root inside me.

Your house, asleep still on the waterfront
of an alien continent,
seems not impossibly distant
with nothing between but desire
and the empty curve of the sea.

Your face clings to my face like a mask.
If I lick my lips, it's your lips my tongue
still tastes. And how different the world appears
through the hazel filter of your eyes.
A strand of your hair strays across my face
and across an ocean I catch its faint scent.

Anticipating spring

Proved February's only cloudless day.
Begun along Crete's rock-strewn southern shore.
In the third bay, outstripping me, you gave
your body to the water inch by inch
till there was nothing but a floating head.
While I, no more than knee-deep, naked,
waited to receive with outstretched towel
a winter Venus rising from a foamless sea.

Lunch in the fields. Lost in the hills all afternoon.
By night the plateau and the long road home.
A waxing moon, too fat now for success,
pursued bright Aphrodite down the sky
while snows of the White Mountains snatched his light
and flung down icy darts that seared our cheeks.

Sleeping, not leaping

Doors, shutters open wide, curtains undrawn.
Dawn light, filtered through cloud-gauze, reflected
off the framed square of southern sky,
wrenched apart my eyes' sleep-sealed lids
and on the balcony parapet your sneakers,
side by side, rang the alarm, suggesting
someone had just stepped out of them.

My mind raced to Sappho's Leap
and your own contingency plans.
But I found you behind me
breathing softly as a baby,
the left shoulder of your shift still holding
        the colour of the night sky.

Travelling alone

Everywhere I go, I thought,
misquoting a Seferis poem,
Greece disappoints me.

The error no mere error
but born of self-deceit, for here
it is I who disappoint myself.

And thus, in her harsh light,
everywhere I travel (translating
more or less correctly now)
Greece keeps wounding me.

Familiar predicament

A fritillary, once brilliant black and orange
but faded now to various shades of brown,
is feeding on a giant thistle-head,
maintaining a precarious balance
by the spasmodic flexing of its wings —
pierced, torn and frayed. Our wings wear out
        before our appetites.

These places

Dusty tracks that run among untended olive groves
and cultivation terraces whose stonework holds
not only soil, but centuries of labour
in their making and maintaining — abandoned now —
and ruined buildings: the roofless walls
of shepherds' huts; whole villages the victims
of remote or recent tremors;
and ancient temples, palaces and theatres.

I come back again and again to these places,
to walk these dusty roads. Not to escape —
the radar installations on the summits
and the headlands see to that —
but to puzzle over something, something
not entirely personal, something
that will never quite declare itself, here
where Europe began . . .
                       where Europe ends,
for beyond the southern coast of Crete
the Libyan Sea, North Africa, Islam
and a thirst for power more vigorous
less senile than our own.

TV in Vietnam in 2012

Here you can watch
non-stop films from Hollywood,
all-day CNN
and hours of *Tom and Jerry*.

Sipping coffee
(a smart café in Nha Trang),
I catch *The Clash of Titans* —
just the last few scenes.

Tom and Jerry seems more apt —
the crafty mouse
who always gets the better
of the greedy cat.

Platonic manikins, Athens

These frozen and idealized forms
of the almost infinitely various
living bodies who might buy
and wear the goods that they're displaying
seem, beneath the season's styles
(loose draped, close fitting or stretched
tight across their creamy smooth
immaculate unyielding flesh),
to be offering — to those of us
constrained by gender to inhabit
clothes of an altogether different cut —
themselves.
               And though there's nothing they
could do for me and precious little
I could do with them, I can't help trying
to imagine what it would be like
to hold one in my arms and feel
those brittle plaster nipples — which,
through fabric, window glass and eyes,
impinge already on my nerves — indent
        my gross material reality.

Hypertension

A minor accident some weeks ago:
my wife in a kayak, me trying to launch
it in the waves, which flung it back against
my shin, at Kókkina Nerá — "Red Waters".
Not red though from my blood — the bruising
severe, but the skin not evidently broken.

And now, quite suddenly, my lower leg
was swollen painfully, and hot and throbbing.
Walking was getting difficult. I hobbled round
to Princeton Hospital and soon was sitting
in a small office with the triage nurse.

Late twenties I would guess. No uniform
concealed her very real attractions, which
she herself was only too aware of.
She examined my unattractive leg
and took my blood pressure. "It's rather high,"
she said, and added, brazenly, "But that
may just be pretty-nurse syndrome."

She must have had to deal with many cases,
but I didn't ask her what the treatment was.

They thought the other thing was cellulitis.
Antibiotics would soon sort it out.
The one they gave me wasn't right, I later learned:
short-term relief of symptoms, certainly,

but then recurrence back at home in Belfast.

At least there was no bill from Princeton Hospital
for curing neither of my two afflictions.

The difficult syntax of love

Love is a verb without a future tense
that can be used at all reliably.
The imperative is therefore suspect too,
and even the infinitive can find
itself in compromising situations,
when subordinated, for example,
to other verbs like "promise" or "expect".

Both the subjunctive and conditional
may be employed in certain circumstances.
The reflexive's safe but may prompt disapproval.
The passive fosters dangerous delusions,
and all past tenses may give rise to doubt.

And though considered transitive
if often singularly fails
to govern or to act upon its object.

Plateia Varnava, Athens
(June 2012)

The square is named for Barnabas, *Saint* Barnabas
I think, companion of that erratic moralist
Saint Paul — "better to marry than to burn".

I used to eat here often years ago
but never clocked it as a pick-up place
for prostitutes. Maybe it wasn't, then.
Now it's the fifteen-centimetre heels
that give the game away.

The first of the well-heeled ladies that I see
is at her pitch outside an unlit shop
some twenty metres down from where I sit
(my table on the pavement by a restaurant door).

She's strolling to and fro; takes five or six
short steps in my direction, then a pause,
then five or six steps back, another pause,
relaxed and unselfconscious, just as much
a part of the mid-evening scene
as children playing in the centre of the square,
or families eating there beneath the trees.

Her hair light brown, and long, her clothes all blue,
with fashion jeans that stop below the knee,
embroidered top whose tiny mirrors catch
the streetlamps and the lights of passing cars.
A hand bag looped around one shoulder and,
in her other hand, one of those tall square

gift-bags made to take a single bottle.

Another high-heeled lady takes the table
next to mine, with the word *justmarried* stitched
right across her backside in heavy sparkling threads.

A man of sixty-some in shorts and sweatshirt
with multicoloured stripes like barrel rings
stretched out across his more than ample belly
stops at the door to ask her name.

"Rosa" she tells him with a well-rolled R,
and that's enough for now — he goes on in.
It's just a trade name though, for in a minute
out comes a waiter with a loaded tray
and seeing her says "Hi, Eleni"
(the solidarity of service trades).

Mercifully she takes no note of me
observing her. I'm just not in her league —
an ageing foreigner in faded clothes.

Her elaborate ear-piece mobile's working hard
and soon a car appears, an older woman
at the wheel, and whisks her off to some assignment
more up-market, I would think,
than this poor square can offer.

> *The café in Éyina*
> *where I am writing this next day*
> *has been invaded by two dozen*
> *well-fed pilgrim ladies, who,*

while waiting for their ice-cream sundaes
and massive plates of sticky cakes,
pass round to sniff at pleasurably
some long white aromatic candles
that one of them's just bought to light in church.

Two more arrive together in a car —
the same high heels, the same gift bags for wine —
and walk off arm-in-arm around the far
side of the square, out of my field of vision.

Focussed on them, I miss the pick-up
of Miss Blue. She's walking past me now
and chatting amiably with a man —
could be a shopkeeper or artisan
just closed his business for the night,
approaching fifty at a guess —
headed no doubt for some nearby hotel.
And silently I wish them well — wish he
may properly appreciate the undoubted
loveliness of her body, and that she
may have at least the satisfaction of
a job well done, a customer well served,
a fee well earned, for surely there's an art
to performing sex for money — an art that might
perhaps, where it exists, be honoured more
(though not of course by Barnabas or Paul).

The swallows of Kastoria

For Yasmin, Makedonissa

Moving among man-planted planes
that line the lakeside road, I find myself
surrounded suddenly by swallows.
Dozens of them swirl around me
faster than the wind-blown autumn leaves.
Leaf-scattered light catching
their blue-black iridescent tails
and skin-coloured vulnerable breasts.
I stand, entranced and mutely honoured
by their absolute neglect of me, until
a blind car passes and they vanish.

I'd seen them in yesterday's dusk,
mistaking them at first for bats:
black shapes restlessly darting, stitching
the narrow scraps of darkening sky stretched
between the rooves of furrier's crumbling mansions;
then in the morning noticed everywhere,
glued into angles under eaves and balconies
and overhanging upper floors, their nests
constructed out of mud and straw.

And in one mansion, lovingly restored,
I met a single swallow, trapped,
drawn back repeatedly to the bright light
of the *kióski* ("summer parlour"
of the handbook, "pavilion" of the dictionary) —
two tiers of windows above cushioned seats
around three walls, the north side arched but open

99

to the *doxatos* (the main reception hall),
the upper windows glazed and mostly screened
with plaster-of-Paris arabesques
inset with glass of many colours,
each panel different, recently remade
("In Turkey," the guide apologized),
the lower, barred and shuttered but not glazed.

Surprised repeatedly against
the same clear pane, the swallow, resting always
from its frantic flight in the same
corner, perched above a plaster screen,
indifferent to the painted trees
aligned before its eyes along the cornice mould,
and painted flowers, is unconsoled
to find itself in what must be
one of the loveliest, most restful rooms in Greece.

The quick and the dead

We arrive too late, to find
most of the guests already left.
And the gardens will be closing in an hour.
The funeral, they say, was very dignified,
the flowers, as we saw, exquisite,
and the pale winter sun exactly
what the occasion and one's sentiments required.

"Come, take my arm and let's at least
walk the length of this pink gravel path
between the two dark lines of sleeping trees,
pause at the end to watch the golden carp
in their over-ornamented fountain pool."

The carp are hard to see at first
in the brown water flecked with dust,
shielded by floating leaves. But there! —
A tinge of colour. A sudden graceful movement.
A quivering stillness just as suddenly resumed.
Another flick of the tail and it thrusts
down into the weeds and is gone.
A flash of recognition in the groin.
I sense the fish as phallus broken free
of the clumsy encumbrance of a body,
the torn end frayed into a fan.

"I don't know why we think the dead
expect of us such dreary, formal clothes.
I never saw you dressed this way before,
nor you me, I suppose."

Odd we should have met so in a graveyard,
after all these years. And both of us
arrived too late, except for one another,
to come on here together,
missing the reception too.

"Shall we walk back now
and let them shut the gates behind us?"

I sense today is far
from being wasted if it find us,
for each other, quick, still, among the dead.

. . . and I, I lie alone

The bedside table: a candle
and a quartz alarm clock;
a film of dust; a small
brass Buddha; and a tube
of ointment for cracked skin.

A double bed; a single
pillow; beside the pillow
a heap of half-read books:
my promiscuous reading.
Four o'clock; rain on the skylight.

Alone in my wide bed
and thinking of you, alone
in your wide bed and thinking . . .
. . . asleep most likely . . .
and all the cold, wet streets between.

London winter evening:
linked verse

Hours pass warily,
staring at the table
with paper spread to catch
words dripping from the pen.

In this room a woman
and two men sit holding pens
and I don't care
which one of them I am.

A fool, he asked
"Who am I?"
A disembodied voice replied
"There is no one for you to be."

Dredged the bottom
of my heart —
found only the broken leaves
of the umbilical conundrum.

Leave the warm ashes
to their soundless dancing
no use straining
to hear the whispering of leaves.

The surprise
of long-dead children
sprouted from the black damp soil
to drown in a pool of sunshine.

Sunlight through a spider's web
the fabric of speech
and Ariadne's thread
a hopeless tangle.

No way out and no way in
for children playing carelessly
beside the gate
with golden string.

In the faded gold
of a winter sunset
nothing so alive
as the skeletons of trees.

The million black fingers
of these tall and silent trees
smooth out the wrinkled surface
of my brain.

Lose your eyes among them.
See there the blood twisting
in the empty whites
of winter evening skeyes.

The journey to Asine

The bus from Galatas was packed
with restless chattering schoolgirls going back
to mountain villages. Then almost empty
for an hour as far as Epidaurus
where it stopped to pick up tourists
bound for hotels in Nafplion.

My route turned off before the town
and I got out to walk the last
few miles on hot and glaring asphalt
with lemon groves on either side,
some open to the road, some fenced
with chain-link and barbed wire, some
screened by bamboo, all edged of course
with the detritus of fast food and drink
tossed out from passing cars.

The first signboard referring to my goal
was unpropitious, since "Ancient Asine"
figured only as the site of "New Bungalows
Ingrid" (the nineteen-twenties' excavations
of the citadel were Swedish too).
Next came "Camping Kastraki. On the beach
of Ancient Asine". Right on the beach,
the long wide-open beach from which the king's
ships, anchored in a vanished harbour, once
set out for Troy, if that *one word* in Homer
may be believed. And as for me, I might
as well have been among *his children, statues,*
as car after car swept past without a glance.

Safari drive, Uganda

The brains of giraffes
are too far above the ground
for us to imagine
what goes on in there.

They inspect us
from the relative security
and detachment
of an upstairs window.

Unless alarmed
they glide by in slow motion
serenely indiff'rent
to bipeds in their tins.

But warthogs
we think we understand.
Like us they're either sleeping,
eating or in a hurry.

They charge across the road
without a glance,
a mother, a baby
and two adolescent males.

The adolescents start to fight
forehead to forehead
attempting to engage
their curling tusks.

The little one,
overcome by its excitement,
spins round twice
then jumps straight up into the air.

But when we stop
to watch a group of buffalo,
one by one they turn
till they're all watching us.

Mahoma Falls

We reach the village with no problem
but there the guidebook drops us.

Other tourists returning to their vehicles
set us on the right path down.

We fall in with a troupe of children
headed towards the river, armed
with empty plastic jerry cans
which the smaller ones will find quite
difficult to drag back up again once filled.

At the Crater Lakes

Two tall trees stand
side by side at the water's edge,
one in full foliage,
the other dead, bleached, bare.

Our dawn descent to the lake —
the sun touching
only the treetops —
disturbs a troop of monkeys.

Those on the ground
make aggressive feints towards us.
Those in the trees
start pelting us with guavas.

The road along the crater rim
has cut through a grove
of what I take (wrongly)
to be cycads,

recalling
that near here
was the world's largest cycad forest,
cut down last year to make a dam.

Long dusty road
punctuated
by the sweet smell of guavas
lying, fresh fallen, in the sun.

The path up to our hut
is littered with them,
discarded, part eaten,
by profligate monkeys.

In the dark you can't help
but crush them underfoot,
releasing the sharp scent
of fermenting fruit.

— ◆ —

Vast tree stripped bare.
Only this morning
we watched the monkeys make a start
on its lush foliage.

——— ◆ ———

Capitals

Kampala — city of more hills
than Rome, but shorter history,
if history be only what's recorded.

Preparations

Three strides and you're home.
The blood is wondering.

Put buckets out to catch the drops —
the notes that she is singing at the window.

The door? It's locked.
Roll up the artificial footprints.

A cup of milk, warmed at the fire,
a string of beads, a drop of blood,
ash of a cypress twig, burned in a silver cup.

Now drink — the gentle potion
of a blue-eyed witch.

Friend in despair

He lies and moans. He sighs
and screws his hands into his face.

There is nothing I can do
but sit here across the room
listening intently
to the roaring of the stove.

"I wish somebody'd shoot me."

But I don't have a gun.

"I've just had it."

Outside a cat howls once
and nothing happens.

Nightmare

After the child, no more of me
took root in her, and kisses slid
from skin like drops of mercury.

Desire, desperate, clutched a tepid corpse,
whose occupant had now withdrawn
into the spare room for the night.

I woke then in the middle of an act
of intercourse, but woke inside the dream.
Another of her lay beside the two of us
and laughed. The one I lay on turned
into a flattened image, with empty
frightened eyes, and slowly faded out.

The Pilgrims' Way
(postcards from Kent)

At breakfast, two rabbits on the lawn,
aware of me but unconcerned,
knowing about glass and the doubtful
reality of what's behind.

— ◆ —

"Beware, Dog" is all the notice says.
Beware, Dog, for the human bite
is sharper than its bark.

— ◆ —

And is the village cross inscribed as well
"to the memory of all those from this parish
who *will give*" — but for what? — "their lives
in the *Next* Great War"? . . . "Lest
we *be not here to* forget."

— ◆ —

On its back in the gutter
where the road crosses high
above the motorway
a dead thrush with its eyes
cemented in horror and surprise.

— ◆ —

Sun and Sunday morning
bring out the men with guns.
Shots clatter round the hills after rabbits.
But the first one that *I* meet on the road
knows at a glance I'm not the shooting type.
It crosses right in front of me
with no sense of urgency
and on the other bank resumes its foraging
while I stand a few feet off and watch.

I walk the backroads of my mind
a much as these damp lanes
where you might hear me muttering
aloud — stitching on the fabric
of this half-imagined world
(so lightly observed)
a faint embroidery of sound.

Two caryatids supporting
just inside the garden gate
the tiled roof of a porch
stand with their backs to me
and stare, I imagine, longingly
at the house they'll never enter;
and offer the undoubted beauty
of their breasts to other,
unresponsive eyes.

Too many kissing-gates
on Footpath two-one-three
and Foothpath two-one-four
through the immaculate
grounds of the manor.
And no fun
with no one to kiss
and having to unsling your pack
each time to get through.

My pack and clothes
in various shades
of faded green
I'm scarcely seen
against these hills
where the new shoots
just begin to push back
the bleached straw of summer
in this far too early spring —
the disturbed seasons . . .

Something like the ghost of a rabbit —
a wet patch of black mud
glistening at first like any other
on the road's hard surface.
But here and there a tuft of fur
and the faint suggestion of legs
and those long ears.
And then, quite clear,
delicately outlined in the mud
like the ring of a bubble just burst
the empty socket of an eye.

— ◆ —

The huge, turf-cut cross of yellowish chalk
that reaches back into the body of the hill
"commemorates the dead of two World Wars".
From the railed enclosure "the memorial stone
has been removed", replaced by a wooden seat
whose metal plaque, surprisingly, quotes Hemingway —
his odd understatement that "the world
is a fine place and worth fighting for".
One agrees, knowing better now perhaps
than Papa Hemmingway just how
uncertain the outcome of *that* battle is.

— ◆ —

Gliders
turning so slowly in the air
seem almost more beautiful
than birds, but,
despite their great size,
much more fragile.

— ◆ —

Church (rems of) by the lake
"remains a consecrated building
and the churchyard is holy ground",
with its tombstones (rems of) — flat slabs,
the grass drawing, very slowly, a final
curtain across their faces,
leaving inscriptions ever more cryptic:
"Thy earthly part . . . blest soule enjoyes . . ."
"The body . . . who died . . . of May . . .
leaving to sonnes by Mary his wife, Nicolas . . ."
". . . eightene years . . . thy body sleeps . . .
wherein our God shall come . . ."
But here I must be careful, for this church (rems of),
"this ancient house of God", is in the care
of "The Friends of Friendless Churches", who warn
of DANGER to "persons playing with the tombstones"
and "will not be held responsible for any injury".

— ◆ —

I don't think March would have been
high season for pilgrims,
slipping and sliding on this muddy bloody path.
But the best of them had horses I suppose
and kept their hands and noses out of it
sitting up there with their tall stories.

— ◆ —

"Whosoever thou art that enterest this church . . ."
I was ready to take off mud-clogged boots in the porch
and enter as into a mosque, but the door
with its familiar invitation to prayer was locked.
I peer instead through clear diamond panes, surprised
by the fresh colours on the walls — recent, unfinished even —
where Christ is calling Kentish fishermen
aboard their boats to follow him, or stands, baptized,
in a narrow, obviously English stream,
attended by what I take to be portraits
of the congregation in their current dress,
in a winter landscape hinting at Breughel.
And one, brighter star in the night portion of the sky
indicates the tin roof of a large open-sided shed.
A woman, pale and beautiful — the artist herself perhaps —
with one delicate hand extended in uncertain gesture
looks down sad-eyed from the pointed window of a tower
as doves gather on the barn behind.
She alone looks out of place, as though observing
from a great distance in time.

    Poem for the countryside — impossible now —
    its beauty — harsh or soft — its traditions.
    The very word *countryside* stinks — not of manure
    but the cheap perfume of the travel brochure,
    the phony poetic for the fake place.
    Write against it, rather, with your head down,
    following a trail of squashed frogs.

— ◆ —

Half a Cornish pasty in the mud.
Point down. Mouth up.
Still fresh. Almost inviting.

— ◆ —

"The Barn Farm Shop"
offers "Farm Produce"
and announces
an "Auction of Promises
(with beer and refreshments)".

— ◆ —

"Words don't really exist. They're all in the mind."
Overheard in the The Chequers, a "Seventeenth
Century Inn for Good Food and Fine Ales".
At first I took him for a business man,
and perhaps he is, though it seems he's working
on a novel, or a play, for he says
to his lunch companion, a much younger man,
"I just spent the weekend in front of a screen.
Now there's an interesting question —
D' you see the hardware or the software?
My wife saw me sitting at the computer,
but as far as I was concerned
I was in a world of my own,
creating characters . . . situations."
But I want *my* software to stay soft,
in a half-light where words really do exist.

— ◆ —

I fight through a wasteland of twigs
sprouted from the stumps of harvested oaks
stretching their spindly arms across a path
already noisy with dead leaves
and deadly with tripwires of bramble.
Out on the open track again I find
red lines on the backs of my hands
black lines on the sleeves of my shirt —
       lines written by twigs.

————◆————

'twixt earnest

& joke

poems

for Alison's eyes

I asked a thief to steal me a peach:
He turned up his eyes.
I ask'd a lithe lady to lie her down:
Holy & meek she cries.

As soon as I went an angel came:
He wink'd at the thief
And smil'd at the dame,
And without one word spoke
Had a peach from the tree,
And 'twixt earnest & joke
Enjoy'd the Lady.

William Blake
"Miscellaneous poems and fragments"

The Muse was prescient.
"You won't have *me*," she said
at an early stage
in our negotiations.
"You won't have *me*,
but at least you'll have
your book of poems."

Loins and eyes

The eye, though it sport no accoutrements of gender,
is love's most penetrating organ,
its deepest, softest, most receptive orifice.

Not in lips' mutual devouring
not in limbs' fierce entwinement
nor in loins' proboscis thrust in loins' flower

not in the hand that seizes breast or buttock
not in the reddening lines nails scribe on skin
nor even in the fingers' gentle tracery

not in the cry from levels below language
nor in the shudder that unseats the brain
granting the body full but brief dominion

but in the sustained, unflinching intercourse of eyes
the root, the branch and crown of all desire.

ἃλς ἰόνιος / hals ionios
(Ionian Sea)

> . . . *this little*
> *portrait of him in pencil.*
> *Hastily done, on the deck of the ship;*
> *one marvellous afternoon.*
> *The Ionian Sea all around us.*
> (C. P. Cavafy, "Of the ship")

Thanks, then, to Mister Cavafy, who sailed this sea
a century ago and marked the spot.
We meet, you and I, on the deck of a very small ship,
the Ionian Sea (and our colleagues) all around us.

And thanks to Mister P. who introduced us,
and Harry too, the New York Englishman,
who, caught in the crossfire of our opening exchange,
melted away, leaving only the salt breeze between us.

As on lips I fixed my gaze

*Thy lips are like a thread of scarlet
and thy speech is comely.*

From the harbour (as Durrell would insist)
of Sycorax the witch, Muse *Kalliopi*
bore us across the straits to Forty Saints.

If — I say *if* — it was Love At First Sight,
then, since dark glasses hid your eyes from me,
there was only the tilt of your straw hat
and the shape of your lips to Fall In Love with —
strangely expressive lips which seemed to speak
two languages at once, their rapid movements
not all translated into words my ears
could hear: your lower lip's facility
in curving up to meet the other only
in the centre, as if to frame some two-
pronged phoneme that belongs to no known language.

So in Albania

Thou hast ravished my heart,
my sister, my spouse;
thou has ravished my heart
with one of thine eyes.

Butrint: the visit to the site and now
lunch beneath the trees. Arriving late
you take the only place remaining —
at the head, where the shade allows
you to remove your hat and glasses.

So in Albania I first see your eyes.

Is an old Muse any less inspiring?

Turn away thine eyes from me,
for they have overcome me.

Kalliopi's recent coat of bright red paint
can't hide the many dints in her steel plates.
This Muse is elderly and our own epics
already more than half-a-century run.

"We're not twenty-five any more" or else
"I wouldn't want to be twenty-five again" —
why twenty-five? (it's you who picked that number) —
becomes our conversation's wise refrain.

At fifty-something one can't be so impulsive.
No wonder then it took my ageing heart
a full one-point-five seconds
from the moment I first saw your face
revealed in all its hard-won beauty
to register the mortal wound —
not from young Cupid's arrow, but your eyes.

Sail on from Bougainvillea

Let her kiss me with the kisses of her mouth
for thy love is better than wine.

It was, I realize now, the first moment
we had been alone together.
We'd left the table, the others gone,
and, as we stood to say Goodnight
in a lighted alleyway beside
the restaurant — the Bougainvillea
with all its bougainvillea — at last
I kissed you, a little awkwardly perhaps,
three times, not quite full on the lips.

Neither too forceful nor too tentative,
I hope, those kisses. It was my mind
that kissed you — mind, heart, soul — kissed *you* and not
your lips or cheek or (had three been four or five . . .)
your nose, your ears, your neck, your eyes
(disturbing your mascara).

Kisses returned? Or, if not returned, accepted then?
You didn't shy away or show surprise,
but then our lips already — at your prompting —
had been sipping from the same small glass of grappa.

In these three days your face has slowly
filled my mind. Your *face* — not trying
to imagine what clothes conceal; your eyes for now
the limit of my sensed desire — to gaze, be gazed at,
eyes to eyes, to sink into your eyes' brown gold.

Love is an exchange of faces, conducted
through the eyes. The image of your face, constructed
from a thousand frank or stolen glances,
moves, breathes, speaks, frowns, smiles *behind* my eyes.
Now, if you will, now take possession
    for this face of mine is yours.

O Snail!

Thy lips, O my spouse,
drop as the honeycomb;
honey and milk
are under thy tongue.

Now *we* have kissed.
Your lips opening, moving
at the touch of mine.
And though we were standing
(by the steps of your hotel)
my eyes had closed
and I seemed to be one
with the damp earth, staring
supine at the stars.
My lips a crevice
explored by this exquisite
soft-shelled bivalve
whose gentle probings
promise to awake the dead.

So nail your courage
to the sticking-place . . .

(Lady Macbeth misquoted, but no matter —
the gentle reader'll know the reason why
and Robert Browning's ghost forgive the rest.)

> *Her hands are as gold rings*
> *set with the beryl.*

Past midnight when we left the table,
the deep colours, richer shadows
of that quiet, displaced Venetian Square,
and walked through sleeping alleyways,
washing still dangling in the warm night air.

A few late stragglers in the cafés
by the Esplanade, where a face from Fayoum
drew me to a jeweller's window.
You followed, missing to begin with
what I had muttered about the portrait
and, looking at the gold instead,
your ringed hand pointing to your unringed left,
"I need a new ring for this hand," you said.

Was it that night (earlier at supper)
or was it next day over lunch
we talked of all the few proposals
of marriage we had made (yes, both
of us) and, in your case, received?
And when was it you confided that
for you Mistress was the ideal role?

Next morning (this, I think, is certain)
we went shopping for your ring. Our tastes
attuned, your decision not too difficult
(there were only two you really liked)
and you emerged with an expensive
jewelled Byzantine wedding band,
but on the middle finger — leaving
the third still free — of your left hand.

"Now we should go buy you a ring,"
you said, as holding hands (my right,
your left), we went in search of coffee.
Now, how I'd love to know just what
was in your mind. But my reply,
somewhat tangential, created
an unfortunate diversion, talking of
the ring I'd lost, and which one day
I'd get a jeweller to remake —
my father's father's old gold ring:
a bloodstone encircled by a snake.

I'm not sure whose unconscious here
was / is working overtime. Was I
being obtuse then? Do I over-interpret
now? OK, then, no more games —
if you asked me to marry you
I would say YES, although you've told me
that you don't want a husband, and I say
that I don't want a wife. Don't worry, though,
I'd never let you do my washing —
though I would willingly do yours
and your ironing (a task I loathe)

for the sheer delight of handling things
that have known the contact of your skin,
the intimate mute companions of your life.
Look! — our principles need not be compromised:
you could be the husband, I the wife!

Λάϊνος / Laïnos
(Made of marble)

O my dove, that art in the clefts of the rock,
in the secret places of the stairs,
let me see thy countenance, let me hear thy voice.

We sat on a park bench,
overheard, if at all,
only by the sombre marble bust
of Dionysios Solomos,
and discussed the immediate future,
the hours between now and breakfast,
deciding not to spend the night together.

The Hotel Cavalieri had come upon us
far too soon for me, for there
I would — or would I this time? —
have to leave you once again
(this would be the fourth of our Goodnights),
but you suggested the roof terrace
and in my heart the gap-toothed cogs engaged
and a rusty elevator rose
shakily towards the stars.
You enquired at Reception
but the terrace had closed at midnight.
And the lift-cable snapped.
                                    I said,
"Perhaps we could sit *here*," pointing
to the red and yellow armchairs
in the mirrored lobby, "for a while",
but you preferred to go outside

and thus the bench; and somewhere
through the trees the sombre poet
of drowned love and the brief moment
of self-knowledge before death.

You assumed I wanted a "proper goodnight"
and we willingly resumed last night's
exploratory kissing. Where, for you,
did the sensation travel to? For me
it remained still concentrated in the lips,
but you drew back and said that we should stop
before it got too complicated.
Then stupidly I said that as for me
it was already complicated.
True — but you bridled; I retracted,
offered some unconvincing words.

Was it then (damned memory!) or before
we started kissing that you said you *could*
invite me to your room, but didn't think
it was a good idea. I agreed —
in retrospect too readily. It's true
I wasn't ready to "make love" but longed
to lie with you, relaxed, engaged
only in the intercourse of eyes,
and let love make itself. I say this
in explanation of my perhaps, to you,
bizarre (or devious) suggestion
as we approached the hotel steps again
that we sleep together but not make love —
a suggestion you declined.

Σαλόνι / Salóni
(Saloon)

By night on my bed I sought her
whom my soul loveth:
I sought her, but I found her not.

Last night our last lost opportunity
(for now) to share a bed, although tonight
indeed we lie together, skull to skull,
strung out along a narrow padded seat
on the *Blue Bridge* across the Adriatic.

Beneath the unrelenting lights of the saloon
your eyes are covered by a pale-blue sleeping mask
(a bright-red patterned handkerchief round mine).

Blindfold, and without contact, like two half-wrapped
mummies on the embalmer's bench, we spend
our first — and (who knows?) only — night together,
in this floating antechamber to Love's Purgatory.

Σα λιόντισσα, σα λιοντάρι / Sa lióndissa, sa liondári
(Like a lioness, like a lion)

Στην Κιβωτό του Νώε που περίμεναν κλωνάρι,
εσύ η καλή λιόντισσα, κ' εγώ το λιοντάρι.

Σαν έρχεται με φύλλ' ελιάς το άσπρο περιστέρι
εμείς την ζούγκλα μας ξανά μυρίζουμ' στο αέρι.

Και τώρα που τ' άλλο πουλί δε γύρισε καθόλου
πως θέλουμ' να βρισκόμαστε εντός του περιβόλου.

Του είδους μας τα δείγματα εμείς τα μόνα δύο,
σωσμέν' από τον γέροντα σ' αυτό το μέγα πλοίο,

να κάνουμε καινούριο τ' ωραίο μας βασίλειο,
ξανά να χαίρουμε ζωή στον ίσκιο και στον ήλιο.

[Literal translation]
On Noah's Ark, where they were waiting for a branch,
you were the good lioness, and I the lion.

When the white dove comes with the olive leaf
we smell once more our jungle in the wind.

And now that the other bird has not returned at all
how we long to find ourselves inside the garden.

Of our kind we are the only two examples,
saved by the old man in this big ship,

that we may make anew our lovely kingdom
to enjoy again our life in sun and shade.

H Ἄλισον της Τροίας / I Álison tis Trías
(Alison of Troy)

Who is she that looketh forth as the morning,
fair as the moon, clear as the sun,
and terrible as an army with banners?

We met (auspiciously perhaps for future voyaging)
aboard a boat between one country and another.
The battered little ferry named for Calliope,
She of the Lovely Voice, the Muse of Epic Poetry.

Where you're concerned, I'm open, certainly, to epic,
but were I to abduct you from South Navarra Drive,
I wouldn't want a thousand ships to put to sea.

A twelve-year siege by Lagan's stream could prove inconvenient
to neighbours in this ten-apartment block, although its name,
Colenso Court Block A, sounds almost worthy of a siege.

No, I would abduct you quietly, avoid publicity
and have the leisure to survey, with you beside me
on the battlements, the greensward and the river,
without the need to dodge Achaean arrows.

Also in sleep

πῆρε στὰ χέρια του ὁ ταλαίπωρος καλάμι

. . . .

νὰ γράψει τί;
        Σεφέρης, «Ὁ δαίμων τῆς πορνείας»

the wretch took in his hands a reed pen

. . . .

to write what?
      Seferis, "The demon of fornication"

Awake now, lying on my back, my hand in sleep
had found, still lightly holds my gently swelling penis.
Is it the dawn, or indigestion, the damp air
streaming through the window, or something else
that's dragged me from my dreams at five a.m.?
. . . *nine p.m.* in Scotts Valley, California,
where, jetlagged, at this very moment it may be
you're turning the key in the door to your apartment.

My mind, too, only half-engorged, I turn,
murmuring "Alison", seeking your face
on an empty pillow it has never touched
and wonder if I'll ever wake to find
your eyes fixed on me, and your skilful author's
fingers priming my reed-pen — to write what?

As in loving, so in Lagan's stream

Many waters cannot quench love,
neither can the floods drown it.

The Lagan flows a hundred metres off
and rowing crews come out to practice early
Sunday mornings. The coach keeps pace on bicycle
and from the far bank shouts encouraging
remarks and orders through a megaphone
directed at my open bedroom window.

"Good. Good. You're moving really well together."
But, sadly, I lie here alone. His words
are wasted on me. "Now, shorten your strokes."
Oh this is rich! I must imagine you
beside, beneath — no, best of all, on top:
I'll have you straddle me — yes, kneeling upright,
moving to the rhythmic thump of eight long oars
striking the water in not quite perfect unison.

"Good. Good. You're moving really well together."
The movement's mostly yours, but *together*, yes,
together's certainly the word for this!
"Shorten the stroke. Yes, Quicker. Quicker. Yes."
You're moving now with eyes fixed on the finish line.
"Yes, that's it. Let her run away." The coach is getting
quite excited now, but something's not quite right:
"Get your body over a bit more," he shouts
and you collapse on me, helpless with laughter,
drenched, both of us, in all the water from the oars.

In so late an hour

Who is this that cometh out of the wilderness
like pillars of smoke,
perfumed with myrrh and frankincense,
with all powders of the merchant?

Tonight I don't think I shall sleep at all.
Your absence from the bed you've never lain in
becomes my engaging and perverse companion,
mutely demanding all of my attention,
ignoring everything I have to say,
as unresponsive as the empty air
to my caresses. But this ghost is yours,
more welcome here than any solid presence,
except of course, αγάπη μου, your own.

The right side of my bed's reserved for you,
but till you come I have to entertain
this inconsiderate phantom in your place.
She prompts desires she cannot satisfy
and peddles stolen icons of your face.

αγάπη μου (*agápi mou*) = "my love"

There is no laptop here

I sleep,
but my heart waketh:
it is the voice
of my beloved that knocketh.

Springfield (optimistic name) Road, Cambridge.
Slept six hours (more than in many days).
Guest in friends' house (no laptop here, no
anxious morning rush to read your evening
email). Waking calm and sure of you
(sleeping now, I guess, six thousand miles
away). Seems that in the night (my night,
but day for you) we've turned a corner —
Spring Field, Scotts Valley: topography
of innocence (all possible) — and you
I believe (oh foolishness!) have (dare
I say it?) opened finally (momentous
word) your heart to me.

ἄλινος θήρα / alinos thera
(a hunt wihout nets)

My beloved put in her hand
by the hole of the door,
and my bowels were moved for her.

Belfast. Thursday the twentieth of June
at two p.m. The Springfield Prophecy
has proved (quietly and undramatically)
to be correct (heart opened, just a crack).
Still ill (you say), you've forwarded the email
that I'd lost. Your fifteen added words
include a new one (new, that is, for us):
"Affectionately" (followed by your name)
seems stronger than the "Love" that ended others.

Progress report (on Saturday the twenty-
second at eight a.m.). Friday morning's message
ended "con baci", and today's (which ends
"*pollá philiá*") begins "My dear . . ." ("How's that
for a start?" you ask). Later, debating mind
versus heart, you write, "If my mind could dictate" —
to your heart, I think you mean — "I would love you
tomorrow." And then, prettily, you add —
silly word "prettily", but my mind
insists on it for now — so, prettily
you add (in brackets) "it's tomorrow already
in Britain." And here my heart soars (ignoring
the conditional, and the fact that Belfast
isn't Britain). Eight hours ahead of you
(where your tomorrow's my today), I'm loved

already! There is more, though: "But we know
from bitter experience how such things go."

Ah! "prettily", I see, pre-echoed "bitterly".

But still, the door *has* opened (just a crack).
The timid girl peers out, and I write back:

Γύρω στα μάτια μου, σαν πεταλούδες,
τρεμουλιάζουν τα «πολλά φιλιά» σου.

     con baci = with kisses

     pollá philiá = many kisses

     The last two lines:

     Yíro sta mátia mou, san petaloúdes,
     tremouliázoun ta "pollá philiá" sou.

     Around my eyes, like butterflies,
     your "many kisses" flutter.

As I long

I charge you, O ye daughters of Jerusalem,
by the roes, and by the hinds of the field,
that ye stir not up, nor awake my love, till he please.

As I long for your heart to open
and the timid girl to creep out,
for her eyes to caress my face,
her fingers to sing in my flesh
and her lips to wander freely
the somnolent landscape
of my body — to stir not up
nor awaken *my* love till *she* please,

so I also long, when *she* please,
to feel in my fingers buds harden
and taste on my lips the salt of her oyster.

's I alone again?

I opened to my beloved;
but my beloved had withdrawn herself,
and was gone:
my soul failed when she spake:
I sought her, but I could not find her.

This morning there's no message from you
and of course (*off* course) I think the worst.
You've nothing more to say. Suddenly,
for you, it's over. You've woken up.
Or last night in the street or on the bus,
you met a stranger's eyes, and your world
turned upside down and I fell off.

Or else my message yesterday offended you.
Was it my intemperate question, then?
You'd written lightly that, having tried
Mahler and fiction, your "old age
would be a profusion of Mozart
and poetry". Lightly I replied,
"Your old age sounds wonderful. May I
share it with you?" I thought to delete
the second sentence, but knowing that,
lightly written though it was, I meant it
in all seriousness, I let it stand.

Are you stunned now by the implications
and unable to respond? That's my best
interpretation of your silence.
And you will write eventually

and tell me that I mustn't say such things
and I'll know we're back on course towards
uncharted regions that you know about.

As I only noted cursorily at first

She brought me to the banqueting house,
and her banner over me was love.

July the first, and, inevitably, I'm remembering
the first of June. Today a train, this time a month ago
a boat. "By any criteria," my diary entry
for that day begins, "the best day for a long time."
A serious understatement *that* seems now,
but lower down there is an even greater one:
"The other highlight of the day" — the first recorded
highlight was Butrint itself: "utterly beautiful
wooded hill that houses the remains of a Greek,
then Roman, then Byzantine city" — "The other highlight" —
embarrassing to transcribe this now — "was meeting
[name redacted] translator (from French)
who lives in San Francisco and knows Greek."
How matter-of-factly the first record
of our meeting starts: "Talked to her on the boat over . . ."
but then I add "in hat and sunglasses" and after
the word "hat" a little sketch, its shape in outline.
The next sentence begins to suggest the meaning
of these details: "Didn't see her face till lunch,
after the trip around the site." Some initial
impressions too embarrassing to repeat
and then, "The attraction is in her face. I felt it
even with hat and sunglasses. But at lunch,
sans hat, sans glasses, I found it hard to take
my eyes off her." And then I note, "We were not
near enough to talk," and draw a crude plan of the table.
At one end, an X in a circle and the word αὐτή.

149

Four (numbered) places off, on *her* left side, against
another X, the word εγώ. Αυτή, εγώ:
between these two terminals the alternating current's
flowed, voltage mounting steadily, these thirty days.

αυτή (*afti*) = she   εγώ (*egó*) = I

In solaria

My beloved spake, and said unto me,
Rise up my love, my fair one, and come away.

This time yesterday
I was talking to you in your bed,
in a darkened room,
the dawn just pushing though the shades,
from a parked car in a London street,
afternoon sunlight through the trees,
an ocean and a continent
between car and bed.

If I were to cross the ocean
and you the continent,
we could meet, as I suggested,
in Philadelphia, the city of
sisterly love (*my sister, my spouse*),
and I could talk to you in bed.

Ναι, σ' όλο τον κόσμο σε γυρεύω
Nai, s' ólo ton kósmo se yirévo
(Yes, through all the world I seek for you)

There are threescore queens,
and fourscore concubines,
and virgins without number.

I sit in a train
staring at your picture.
You stare back at me
from six years before we met,

just perceptibly younger
than in the photos
that I took of you in Greece
four weeks ago.

But in all of those
your eyes are either closed
or hidden by dark glasses,
or you look aside.

The problem posed
by your "infinite variety" —
are all these various aspects
your one face?

Lunch at Liá,
you in three-quarter profile
(a surreptitious close-up shot)
pensive, distante,

et distinguée,
but difficult to reconcile
with memory,
or your smiling swimsuit self.

Your account of your own life's the same
but there the photos
start from age one
and run to forty-six.

1963
the schoolgirl aboard a liner,
who, I can just believe,
but cannot see, is you.

1973
a bridge in Leningrad,
hands in pockets, smiling,
the soft bloom of youth,

and I can recognize,
even in a still,
your lower lip's
familiar questioning quiver.

Aged twenty-five exactly,
a certain hardness
(or is it perhaps sadness?)
tightens your face.

'78, in Epidaurus,
smiling again
alone in the theatre's
tiered seating,

your eyes completely hidden
by your fringe,
whose severe line parallels
the top of your Greek dress.

'82, Bulgaria,
happy among friends
but your shades
deprive your readers of your eyes.

'88, your face is rounder,
hair much shorter,
a child clings to you:
practical; a mother.

Strangest of all to me,
spring '93:
husband, boat and you
looking much more *gamine* than wife.

Was it only
between then and '96
that you became
the person I begin to know,

who from the first page,
utterly beautiful at last,
completely self-possessed,
smiles back at me?

pensive, distante, et distinguée, = pensive, remote, and elegant

gamine = a slender, elegant young woman with a touch of mischief

No aisle for Alison?

Thy cheeks are comely with rows of jewels,
thy neck with chains of gold.
We shall make thee borders of gold
with studs of silver.

The other ring (the one you didn't buy),
smaller, more delicate, an almost heart-shaped
sapphire set in fine gold filigree, after you'd left
the island — or, rather, since we left together,
after *I* had returned to Kerkyra alone —
I bought for you.
                              Rings can't be sent. Its box
sits on a shelf above my desk. Each time
I prise the tight-sprung lid, it seems
to have become more beautiful, the gold
paler, more subtle, and the sapphire glows
a deeper blue.
                              In one scenario
I just hand you the box — a simple gift,
from friend to friend. "A souvenir," I say
"from Kerkyra." You open it. You smile.
And then, with studied carelessness, I add
"And if ever you agree to marry me,
we'll call it your engagement ring. I don't
intend to buy another one, you know."
But your response is missing from that script.

In the shorter version of the scene
I don't produce the ring until I've asked
the fateful question, and you've answered, "Yes."

Alison + I

Eat, O friends; drink,
yea, drink abundantly,
O beloved.

Alison + I = *ailinos*,
a plaintive dirge to ancient Greeks.
No, that won't do. I'll try again.

Alison + I = *liaison*.
Ça c'est mieux. Mais pas trop dangereuse,
je vous en prie. Hein! pourquoi pas, alors?

Mais soyons nous un peu plus objectifs:
me + Alison = a text message:
"meal is on". Eat, drink and be merry then?

For tomorrow — here comes the *ailinos* — we die.

Lines 4–6:
That's better. But not too dangerous,
I beg of you. Huh! why not, then?

But let us be a little more objective:

Ars is longa, vita's brevis

Set me as seal upon thine heart,
as a seal upon thine arm:
for love is strong as death.

We die; the store of our experience is dispersed,
and, as it blows away, some scraps, like rags in trees,
are caught, briefly, in others' memories; *they* die
and nothing then remains but what we chose
to mould in clay or cast in bronze;
to represent in line or colour
on paper, wall or canvas; to encode
on staves for instruments or voices yet unheard;
or to delineate in strings of words
to enter minds as yet unborn.
This is our only immortality
blindly entrusted, of necessity,
to persons unknown, unknowable.

As we have learned, in part, to form ourselves
of image, music, word, produced around us
or left by those already gone,
so do we have through "art" our own
small opportunity to add
our shards to the untidy heap
that constitutes our foolish species'
supposèd understanding of itself
and its domain — this lovely, ill-loved islet
in the cold ocean of infinity —
as I now add these poor half-humorous
attempts to un-defend myself against

the human, individual and only *love*
that moves the sun and other stars.

Loans I never could repay

Behold, thou art fair, my beloved,
yea, pleasant: also your bed is green.
The beams of your house are cedar,
and your rafters of fir.

In these four nights in your small house
in California, I have become
your lover, but I do not think
you love me yet. I sense through all
your injured wariness the soft,
slow motion of your heart's rotation,
and wonder if I'll hear some tell-tale
click, when — if ever — it should lock
on the trajectory that leads to mine.

Once wounded so, it's harder now
to give your heart again. Then *lend*
your beauty, body, mind to me
to be redeemed when you so choose.
Reserve your heart until you have
explored and tested, proved, accepted mine.

In a solitary deck chair

A fountain of gardens,
a well of living waters,
and streams from Lebanon.
Awake, O north wind;
and come, thou south;
blow upon her garden,
that the spices thereof may flow out.
Let my beloved come into her garden,
and eat her pleasant fruits.

Idling on your deck
in warm midday sun
I lay Bashō by the lemon tree
and close my eyes.

Upstairs your neighbour
is watering her pots
and the drip of the waterfall
lulls me to sleep.

The engine
of the Tree Expert's truck,
running to pump the hose
that feeds another neighbour's trees,

wakes me all too soon
to the complex realities
that sustain
this suburban paradise.

I see why some days
you don't stir
from this leaf-fringed patch of light
scarcely bigger than this deck chair.

May *your* tree flourish,
give lemons for your G 'n' T
and so become
your Tree of Idleness.

Travails on arrival and departure

"FLYING THE FRIENDLY SKIES"

United — well, yes and no —
by United Airlines,
now taking me away
from you again.

BAGGAGE HANDLING

Next time I come
there'll be far less baggage
for you to handle
and you can handle me instead.

SECURITY

Your scan detected
prohibited items,
most serious
the inability to dance.

CUSTOMS

I arrived with caseloads of hope.
You impounded it
but returned a portion
before I left.

Man losing his bearings

Until the day break,
and the shadows flee away,
I will get me to the mountain of myrrh,
and to the hill of frankincense.

Leave in the fog. Visibility low
and getting lower as the bus approaches
the Golden Gate Bridge. Can just make out the wakes
of several small boats headed for the ocean.

Leave, despite the damp air, dry-eyed and calm,
obstinately feeding on your refusals,
daring to think my absence can succeed
where my presence so singularly failed.

I withdraw from my invasion of your space,
hoping my absence may become as palpable
to you as yours was earlier to me
(in rooms you've never seen, may never see)
and haunt you lovingly, a pleasurable
presence, soft-fingered ghost of your apartment.

An' so I learn
some home truths

Who is this that cometh up
from the wilderness?

"After California, Belfast
feels more empty without you
than it felt
without you before.

"Having known your body
it's easier at first
to hold you in my mind
(with more to hold onto).

"But gradually
the photos on the walls
revive, and reassert
your former phantom presence."

— Lines scrawled on *The Guardian*
over lunch, for which I pay
with a local banknote
whose motto reads:

NIHIL IMPOSSIBILE
ERIT VOBIS.
"For you [plural] nothing
shall be impossible."

This is a long-distance call

I called her,
but she gave me no answer.

An hour or more
of loitering in a Cornish lane
at a time
when sensible folk are in bed.

Half the universe
visible above
and a huge sickle moon
just clearing the horizon.

Trying your number
every two or three minutes,
hearing the "busy" tone
in California,

and in between,
the soft liquid calls of owls,
the angry squawk of a crow
disturbed in its sleep,

the excited breathing
of some predator,
the long pathetic death squeals
of its struggling prey,

the leathery flap of bats' wings,
the snuffling of cattle,
or else the silence
ringing in my ears.

At last the ring tone, but then
only your recorded voice —
a new upbeat message
with music.

I left *my* message,
mentioning the lane, the stars, the moon,
and hoping
"to speak to you sometime".

I turned off the phone,
walked slowly to my rented bed,
sure that you were home
but wouldn't answer.

Lady Julian's offering

The keepers of the walls
took away my veil from me.

The Lady Julian of Norwich, whom
I heard discussed this morning on the radio,
in *Revelations of Divine Love* speaks
to all those who "aspire to be
       lovers of Christ".

These words became *my* revelation.
I realized that these three months
you've been the object of my faith
and of my worship, been no less
than my Divinity. I had aspired to be
       a lover of You,

whom I encountered on the road,
not to Damascus, but Butrint.
The photographs that I had framed —
the expense an offering — that now
confront me from the walls, were icons;
and my devotions all the hours I spent
       writing these hymns to You.

But with this revelation,
scales fall from my eyes
and I become once more
AN INFIDEL.

Remnants
of
religion

The hands of God

We're all in the hands of God, you say,
and I, that those hands may crush us any day.

The Word arises from below,
no human-faced Pantocrator
looks down from dome above.
God does not hide behind
the painted images of wall
or screen, but lies congealed
below the church's floor, entombed
beneath the abstract pattern of the tiles.

The Word arising from below
(and subject to attack by worms)
is constantly made flesh
and pitches its intrusive tent
in us, for whom the flesh
might otherwise have been enough,
and drags us screaming into mental life
to last until the day the cold
hard hand of God shall close
around the heart,
and flesh depart,
engraved on stone
the word alone
remain.

A mixed blessing

Annunciation. Implantation of the seed.
By word of mouth. Or overshadowing power.
By breath. Or wind. Or by whatever means . . .

Are angels' wings not feathered white like swans'?
Jacob wrestled all night with an angel.
Why not she? On a straw-filled pallet
in her parents mud-brick house in Nazareth.

Her trembling acquiescence in the sacred game.
Emboldened as the golden shower envelops her.
God become angel become self-consuming fire
dies down to glowing embers in her womb
which her dumbfounded patience must rekindle.

She lies alone now with her secret, knowing
nothing like this will come to her again.
The angel's part, if told, will be hushed up,
Joseph's paternity maintained.

And a sword shall pierce through your own soul also.
These words she will receive within the year
and her heart become a storehouse of sayings.

Klafthmonos Square, Athens,
25th of March 2001

I'm here to photograph the bust of Vlasis Gavrilidis,
a journalist who "wrote with respect for his readers",
but who now suffers from the *dis*respect of those
who almost certainly have never read him
and probably have no idea who he was.
His plinth is covered with graffiti in two languages.
Children have tried to add some colour to his marble features.
Moustache and eyebrows are now orange-brown.
Dark blue's been daubed around and in his eyes.

Today's the National Festival, the anniversary
of the outbreak of the War of Independence. The date
was fudged a bit to coincide with the Annunciation . . .
The birth of the Greek Nation and the birth of Christ —
a powerful association still at work today.
(What chance of peace when God
has got so many Chosen Peoples?)

This is the day for military parades,
the winged Archangel's given way to fighter jets
and here we're in the flight path. Groups of four,
in close formation skim the rooftops of the taller buildings,
pale undersides like pigeons' breasts, their claws retracted,
and weapons slung beneath their wings. Each time they come
the square's own pigeons in the trees and on the edges
of the rooves take to the air in hundreds. Just time
to circle once and settle back into the treetops
before the next four come, and panic starts again.

Gavrilidis did not exactly propagate the Annunciation
for that belongs to Luke, but the *Akropolis*,
the newspaper he founded, dared to publish Matthew
in demotic, the modern "Language of the People",
engendering the Gospel Riots (a century ago
this year) and, on the Feast of the Archangels, Michael
and Gabriel (angel of the Annunciation),
when police and soldiers and some persons unidentified
at upper windows of the Ministry of Finance opened fire,
they left eight men shot dead, another sixty wounded.
It's Matthew of course who has the story
of the Massacre of Innocents.
But who, if anyone, was innocent on that November day
is not by any means an easy matter to decide.

Visitation

The babe leaped in her womb, she thought, for joy;
or looking, was it, through his mother's eyes
into another's eyes and womb, he started —
seeing there the source of all his woes, the one
before whom he'd have to run, straight
into the arms of the other woman in his life,
    who loved him, even unto death.

Strange land: a child's story

You took me away to a strange land
out of the reach of the maddened kings
whose magic mirrors told them of one
whose palace was not made of stone,
whose riches did not shine,
of one who at a distance
would see the ruin of their days.

And you they saw, coiled as a snake within.
And they knew, then, that we should eat the fruit,
that we should eat the fruit and know them,
know them for what they were — dust
in the mind and bitterness,
angry faces in the clouds, whose fate
hangs on the pleasure of the wind.

And they sharpened their knives.

But you took me away to a strange land
where I learned strange songs.
And the people of that land
bowed down to statues
and we bowed with them.

But even as we bowed
with our faces in the sand
you whispered to me "God
is a clown on a bicycle.
He rides through the hills and he laughs."

But I liked the statues. "What you like
you must carry," you warned.
"But I'm strong," I replied and I tried
to carry the statues, I tried
to ride on the bike.

But I never reached the hills.

They brought me back, the companions.
They fed my face to stop my tears.
The made a house for my statues
and on the wall, to comfort me, they hung
bright pictures of the hills and trees.

In the long years of exile
they died, the companions you gave,
the mother without a husband,
the old man in the shepherd's dress.

And you it is who walk beside me
when I walk alone along the road at night.
You it was who lay beside me
here in this borrowed room.

Here in this borrowed room whole days
I've faced the blank wall, waiting,
and now in sleep I felt your body
brush against me whispering, "Why wait?

"You have lain by the stream in the scent of the pines.
You have stood in a walled garden at dusk
and smelled the stars. In the flooded ruins

of a king's palace you have heard frogs sing.
Why wait? — *for they are dead*
which sought the young child's life."

An old man at Midnight Mass

Once again, after long absence,
and perhaps for the last time,
I kneel in this familiar outhouse
to receive on my tongue a morsel
almost without taste
of the broken body of life.

And from the gilt cup, held in another's hands
and tilted, briefly, against my lips,
the dark liquid floods my dry mouth
and turns, inside of me, to fire.

What shall I ask at this midwinter birth,
this star-point of clarity in the rambling dark?
Only this: that spring come, and I see again,
and perhaps for the last time,
on the tree that rubs its limbs against my window
    the dusk-pink flowers unfurl.

A Brief Guide
to the Monastery of Daphni

Enter, if you have to, from the south
(often the only door unlocked)
but don't look up. You were not meant
to see the dome from here. Instead
turn left, walk through into the narthex.
There at the west door turn around
and, keeping your eye-line level,
fixed on the tiny flowers of light
pierced in the alabaster panes
behind the empty sanctuary,
pass through the first arch. Three more steps
and then you can allow your eyes
to glide slowly up the apse wall, past
the blue robes of a headless Virgin
(if you can see her in the gloom)
and gold robes of her headless Child,
the blank apse vault, then Daniel, flanked
by other prophets (some fragmentary)
ranged in a frieze but separated
by the sixteen deep-set
narrow windows of the drum;
then, slowly still, above their circled heads,
across a broad and featureless expanse
of heavily eroded gold,
until, at the apex of the dome,
you finally confront the Face.

Six times life size,
divorced in scale and space

from all the other figures here,
its harsh uncompromising gaze
will not meet yours — the eyes forever
bent towards the left, the side
to which the goats would be consigned
at the division of the flock.
The Face of Christ Pantocrator,
unnaturally lined and sagged by age
beyond its thirty mortal years.
"I and the Father are one,"
John has him say, and you who stand
and strain your neck to see the Son
will see him in a full eclipse —
the patriarchal physiognomy
is overlaid upon, obscures
the much-imagined younger face.

The Gentle Jesus of your childhood,
the white-robed, pained and caring Christ
with gothic lantern in his hand
who stands outside the door and knocks,
even the dozen other Christs
depicted here much lower down
in scenes of earthly narrative
are harmless dreams, beside this awful
Christus of Byzantine nightmare:
image of that dread Judge
before whose presence they believed
they would one day be hauled — knees, bowels
giving way, minds black with fear —
their lives strung out between the threat
of endless torture and the prize

(which in their iconography
is always much less well defined)
of everlasting joy and bliss.
A desperate game, with unpredictable
and shifting rules, but at its end
the Book he holds — still firmly closed —
in one long-fingered, bony hand
(the nail holes now the faintest scars)
would, or would not, they thought, contain
their names and all appeals be disallowed.

That Face which overpowers the church
is Art — the rest just pious illustration.

To the Ayatollah Khomeini : an oblique tribute

I have read in translation a speech you delivered,
some months before your death, to teachers and students,
members of religious institutions,
on the third of Esfand thirteen-sixty-seven.
And from that seamless flow of twisting rhetoric
there fell into my lap, like a diamond
flung from the unravelling turban of a dervish,
one short sentence, startling in its imaginative power.
Speaking of the Shah's time you recalled
how the "ulema and clergy" of your faction
"prepared themselves against all kinds of poisonous arrows
being fired at Islam", and then you declared —
and these are your words as they've reached
across the frontiers of language — "They arrived,"
you said, "at the slaughter-house of love."

"They arrived at the slaughter-house of love."
I saw this sentence poised on your narrowed lips,
like a burning angel emerging
from the dark cavern of the mouth of God,
tiny as the struggling figures of Rustam
and the White Demon on the spine of Rushdie's *Verses*;
poised for a moment before he leapt
across the fourfold abyss of language and culture
and race and religion, over the disjunction
of time and date between us, into my mind,
where, as he grew to full stature,
with a creaking and grinding of rusty hinges
a great door opened and I looked
        into the Slaughter-House of Love.

And there they were, "the World Devourers",
mild mannered, awkward of speech,
with their thin smiles and their pale skin,
proud horses once, between the thighs
of the Spirit of War, now riderless,
their "explosive wrath" all spent
against the towering adamantine walls
      around the Slaughter-House of Love.

And they were there, "the seekers and enthusiasts"
who had "torn away the black breast of ambition"
and, fulfilling their pact "with the white dawn of love",
had "achieved their goal of martyrdom".
But they were small, so small, less than atoms,
not visible to the naked eye,
not though they gathered in their thousands —
so vast this Paradise, so limitless
      this Slaughter-House of Love.

And *the infant girl* was there,
she who was *buried alive*, and when *asked*
for what crime she was thus slain
replied with questions of her own:
Do you burn books, do you cover
the faces of women for the same un-reason?
Is it for fear of the flames that flicker
behind the dark screen of your eyes?
Tell me, is it there
      the Slaughter-House of Love?

I swear by the turning planets
and by the stars that rise and fall
I do not hate your religion
any more than I hate my own,
but I hate all religion when it makes
hatred a virtue, when it sits easy
in chambers of commerce with makers of bombs,
when it "cleanses the jar" in contempt
from which your "own child Mustafa drank water",
when it would rise up and kill to defend
from words printed in books *the Lord of Creation,*
or the Word Made Flesh
        from the Slaughter-House of Love.

O come, let us reason together,
in the name of the Compassionate the Merciful,
untouched by any insults which our mouths can fling,
immune to the "poisonous arrows" of our hearts,
beyond our reach, unknowable, enthroned forever
        in the Slaughterhouse of Love:
when the earth is rocked in her last convulsion
when *each soul shall know what it has done,*
may we not both be victims, you and I together,
        in the Slaughter-House of Love?

Ite missa est

You have shadowed me, O Christ,
with your *un*-Real Presence.
And the Elements failed to contain you.

In the soft light of your Sanctuary
where gilded pillars raised
a canopy above the Table

I have received your Token in my hands,
I have sipped from the Cup and been stung
by the taste that wavers between blood and wine.

(And none must be lost, the dregs drunk,
the Cup washed and the water
poured into the footings of the House.)

It is finished, your Era.
Its far from immaculate
conceptions have released you

from the weight of liturgical robes,
the constant entreaties of the faithful
and the Company of Angels.

The Host no longer
Prisoner of the Tabernacle
or self-dispensed at the Feast.

But the Deposition of the Flesh
left a death's head
staring from the Screen.

Between radius and ulna
and between the metatarsals
the iron spikes still held,

the Crucified still hung there
as a skeleton — all means
of articulation gone —

until the House was shaken
and the bones clattered to the floor,
dissolved into a pool of dust

and there remained only a few rusted nails,
two jointed timbers, an ironic
Superscription, a blurred

and flickering image on a screen
and a voice on a tape loop
endlessly repeating

Ite missa est
Go, the mass is ended
Ite missa est . . .

That other city
(in memory of Deryck Dyne)

Another city shall be found, better than this.
C. P. Cavafy, "The city"

I can imagine with some pleasure
that in another city and in some other time
we might have been neighbours.
                              Not next door,
or down the street, or just around the corner,
but near enough
(if you would go without your beard)
                    to visit in some alley
midway between your house and mine
the same barber's shop.

                    And there
some mornings we'd be bound to meet,
you in the chair next to mine —
things to be said, but we
must sit stiff-necked, and I
can't turn to you or you to me.
We stare instead at those two
white-robed, foam-bearded angels
seated and solemn behind the glass.
Let them be the ones to speak.

And after the soap and the blade and the towels,
after the purification and the message
of the angels, I know a place close by —
it's none too clean perhaps, but quiet and cool

and can provide what's needed for the next stage
of our liturgy . . .
                    where what is . . .
                                        is broken . . .
in that other city.

Pins and needles

The planet shrinks and wingless angels multiply,
doomed to discover by experiment
just how many can go on dancing on a pin.

The rich hate crowds; try by selective breeding
to produce a smaller camel, but realize
the time's too short; invest instead in steel,
commissioning needles dwarfing Cleopatra's.

Preaching with precaution

Above the west door of a city church
in a semi-cylindrical niche,
topped by a tiny key-stone Roman arch,
a half-size statue of Saint Francis stands,
eye-level from the top deck of a London bus.
A second glance reveals the netting,
stretched across the front — to protect the saint
from the attentions of the birds.

Veni creator spiritus

He stood in the early hours in an empty street.
Darkness and silence. Frost and streetlamps.
The houses all asleep, and he, alone, awake.
    It seemed to him for a moment
    that he could have been their Maker.
But then a sudden breath of wind reminded him.
    For he was breathed upon.

A timetrick

There's only one way
from one day to the next —
through the night with eyes
    wide open.

For if you sleep
you'll always wake
the same day as you woke
    the day before.

There's only one way
from one day to the next —
through the night with eyes
    wide open —
that can defeat
the backward slip
    of circling hours.

Confusion

I am not here. I am not here.
Who is not here? He sits cross-legged
upon the bed, voice says "I am not here."

He is not here, whoever speaks.
The mouth, the bed, the legs are mine.
Are whose? — You are not here.

I *am* not here, not here, not now.
I feel a body feels I am not in it.
A room is crying out for me to come.

If I'm to go I must know where I am
and why I *am* not where I feel it knows I'm not.

But sinking to this scribble
at a table, finds no longer sure
that there are two of us.

A hotel room in Chania

I only had that room three weeks
yet every detail's burned itself
into my mind and there remains
for me to visit any time
by simply closing eyes . . .

The furniture I'd rearranged
the day I came — cheap factory stuff
all stained the same dark brown.
The books and papers I had spread around.
The basin that I pissed in in the night.
Two imitation oil lamps with electric bulbs —
not what I'd have chosen, but I grew fond of them,
was grateful for their warm and feeble light.

The multiple and overlapping shadows
of the balcony's elaborate ironwork
thrown up on walls and ceiling by the rows
of evening streetlamps, and the rapid,
subtle changes as the one defective light
across the square flicked off and on.

The morning pattern from the coarse-weave curtains
sinking slantwise down the rough-faced wall as the sun
broke from the mass of rotting buildings to the right
and which, on days when I lay late in bed
I'd watch withdraw, gradually,
across the grey-and-white-flecked marble floor.

— ◆ —

Not just the room but all the square
below the balcony where I ate
breakfast sometimes, sometimes wrote letters
at a table not much bigger than a book
and often leaned against the railings
for half-an-hour together, just watching
what was happening below . . .

Dogs and children climbing on the statue
of the patriarch. Tourists queuing to change money
on the platform of the yellow postal caravan.
Arguments among the taxi drivers at the rank.
And once a demented woman raging
at the world, with her attentive audience
keeping their distance in a circle round her
until an ambulance arrived.

Beggars on the cathedral steps with outstretched hands.
The jerky movements of those other hands
on the face of the cathedral clock, which
from the corner tower closest to my room
struck so loudly one o'clock at half-past
every hour, confusing me in sleepless nights.
Dignitaries and business men who had dropped by
to pay, so briefly, their respects to God
and hurried women who emerged
still muttering their prayers with eyes
cast down against the sudden glare.
October twenty-eighth a military parade —
a shambles but the bishop blessed it anyway.

— ◆ —

Exactly opposite my balcony and facing me
stands Athenagoras the Patriarch.
Stern yet benevolent his face,
not unacquainted, certainly, with grief.
Dignified despite the children and the dogs.
His right arm permanently raised to bless,
the fingers delicately curled to shape
the ancient gesture; and the left
folded across his chest, the hand
not clutching but at rest against the cross
which hangs on its stone chain around his neck.

"I've often wondered in these past few days
what am I doing in this place?
Years I waited for the chance to settle here
but now I ask, why did I ever want to come?

"The city's foreign yes. It has the sea — the mountains
rise behind — and light and heat, the sun
all day at almost any time of year.
The city's small, a hundredth of the size of mine.

"Why should I think that here my mind,
so long confused, will suddenly come clear?
Or fumbling in the hotel corridor —
the lights don't work of course — I'll find
the door where I have shut away my life
and hear at last a voice I recognize as mine?

"And will that voice just tell me that there's no escape?
That this or any city is the same?

That the city is within us? Or we wear it like cloak?
Or it's the air we breathe — the poisoned air
that eats into the fabric of the brain?"

— ◆ —

One version of my life died in that room
Another left it, raw, untried, not knowing
where to go but lighter — so much of what I brought
into that room I left behind. I wonder now
if other guests in that hotel will catch their shins
against those unseen things I left — a mass of guilt,
heaps of regrets, the floor in places more
than ankle-deep in my discarded thoughts.

——— ◆ ———

Ghosts

I wept when I saw the children in the street.
I called them from my window, but they did not hear.
I stretched out my hands towards them
but they did not see. They could not see.
They could not hear. They were beyond reach,
in another world, but not a child's world
and I wept as I watched them passing in the street.

Unspoken

We have the words
but only they the knowledge.
The dead have much to tell us
and no words. Otherwise
they might have told us
and we also could have died.
But we remain, children
slowly sinking in the swamp.

Dramatic fragment

Do we dare to summon you once more onto the stage,
Tiresias, knowing our masks are powerless
to deceive those sightless eyes.
Old man, who have foreseen, *who have foresuffered all*,
heavy with secrets culled from many centuries,
with keener sense than sight you'll read whatever's written
on the dog-eared pages of our souls.

No, come aside and sit with me beside the fire.
Stir the embers and I'll tell you how the sparks fly up.
From patterns I'll describe, tell me, as much
or little as you please, what is and is yet hidden,
or what is still to come. I'll not compel your speech again.
You can return then to the distant future of the ancient dead.

The sick house

He came from a background of dust.
The inheritance was most unpromising —
an old house built round four sides of a spacious court,
two floors of rooms, windows that face both in and out.

The incoherence of that house —
the stairs that end against a wall
or *de*-scend only to ascend again,
blind corridors and rooms that have no light,
an entrance hall impressively conceived
that gives no access to the other parts.

Nothing had stirred inside that house for centuries.
His ancestors had lived out there
their slow deaths, uncomplaining,
and their last breaths still hung,
discolouring the air where they
themselves had faded into furniture.
And words deserting in despair
the pages of the unread books
had gathered on the window ledges
and the floor, on tables and the backs of chairs,
and on the handles of the doors
regrouping in a frantic effort to express
the stifled griefs absorbed for generations,
by the curtains and the paper on the walls.

The inheritance not promising of unlived lives
whose brittle arms extend like twigs
obstructing every passage in the house

and fingers, thornlike, catch at clothes
imploring the return of unfilled hours.
Cramped souls whose hearts had calcified
from the slow seep of unshed tears inside
crowd out all habitable space.
And all the words they never spoke
now gathered in his brain like mice
let loose inside a sack of grain,
devouring all the future's unsown seed.

But first take axe to trees some madman planted —
a hedge of poplars round the house
six feet apart and six feet from the walls
on all four sides, which his successors,
out of strange respect, or idleness, had left
unthinned, unpruned, until the house was choked
and all the outward-facing windows blind.
The trees ingrown into each other's limbs,
their fingers wormed into the stonework
of the walls, their crowns had long outstripped
the ridges of the slated roofs
and all their lower parts were tightly bound
by the convolvulus — its brief white flowers
the only sign of life observable
the only greeting which this grim retreat
afforded to the outside world.

A single opening in the screen of trees
had been maintained, sufficient for a man
on foot, no more, approaching by
the narrow tree-lined drive, to pass into
the space below the vaulted carriage gate

which gave onto the cobbles of the yard.

The burning of the trees goes on for weeks.
Each day he's adding to the fire
more of the chairs and tables, beds and books,
the curtains and the carpets — all the contents
of the house to be consumed — decaying
plaster from the walls, the rotted boards . . .
and with the flames the ghosts rise up
delivered by this funeral pyre from all
the objects into which their lives had sunk.

When all the contents of the house
have been consumed, and when he finds himself,
at last, alone, released from all
that was not him, will nothing then remain?
Or will the silence be broken — a door
opening by itself? And will he be seen
standing in an empty room
where a narrowing band of sunlight
        falls across the floor?

Behind the Veil

The sun is covered by the moon
and to the hill all eyes are drawn
where nails and spear have done their work.
There, outside the gates, the Son,
forsaken by the Father, dies.
And at his last and wordless cry
the moon lets go her grip upon the sun,
the Veil is torn, the Holiest Place laid bare.

But one child only — a boy abandoned
in the chaos of that afternoon —
is there to see that on the Mercy Seat
a woman sits and bleeds. The Ark
of the Covenant beneath is stained —
defiled? — anointed! — with the blood
which, issuing from her womb, flows down her thighs.

The goddess sits. The goddess waits.
The goddess bleeds. For words cares nothing.
Expects no gifts. Accepts no sacrifice.
The goddess sits. The goddess waits.
The goddess looks. And if her eyes
should rest on you, you must return her gaze,
your eyes her eyes hold, by hers be held.
Fall at her feet and you'll be lost
forever in the pattern of the tiles.
Do nothing to remind her of
that immortality she would put off.
And you, put off that cloak of impotence,
those robes of mourning for the life

which is to come. Go, radiant
and smeared with blood, into that hideous night
where dead and living mingle in the street.

Good Friday in Herakleion

Good Friday in Herakleion, Great Preparation
as they call it here, and up he goes again,
the Scarecrow on the Scarecrow's Pole — two thousand years
he's kept the sparrows from the Tree of Life.

And through the streets at night they carry him,
the Scarecrow in the Scarecrow's Tomb — too small by half.
Behind him, schoolgirls in white dresses walk in pairs,
clutching their candles, which keep on blowing out.
Their chant, gone flat and dead now from a hundred
repetitions, is silenced by a gesture
from the deacon in the middle of a phrase.
They stand and shuffle till the traffic cop's shrill whistle
secures the Scarecrow's passage through the cars.

A kind of death

Stretched on the lime-trees of night he dreams
eyes wide open on the dark. And from his eyes
darkness streams into the dark. And through his eyes
black fragments of night creep inside the skull.

The eyes are vacant now, the skull a void
and black is the colour of day.
But what is the colour of the empty space
where the night has dissolved?

Holy Saturday

The journeys of Holy Saturday
in the hidden time between death
and the end of death.

The small roofed boat
that drifts straight and steady
in the dark water under the hill

or the wheels whose slow rotation
carries us over the ground
away from where the body lies
in its gaudy box under the crumbled soil

to a milder land where already
the blossom dances in the bright breeze
or the light faintly shows
at the river's exit from the hill.

The journeys of Holy Saturday
are made also by those
who drove the nails, or forced
the spear in under the ribs,
who shouted for blood
and preferred the thief.

Easter Vigil

Lies sleepless in a concrete barn
the night of Holy Saturday.
The roof of corrugated tin
turns up the volume of the rain.
The body complains of too much
meat and wine; awaits another
resurrection.
    Uneasy sleep
towards dawn. Then the shock
of daylight. Framed in the empty doorway
one of Van Gogh's orchards, alive
with fresh white flowers and the restless
chattering of crows — migrated from
some darker canvas. Shuffles out,
naked as the Risen Christ, grazing
his head on an apple branch
and feeling the sky soft above him
empties his bladder in the grass.

Cracks and hollows in the Rock of Ages

I was in the isle called Patmos
and *on the Lord's day* too, although
not exiled by a Roman emperor.
I heard no *great voice as of a trumpet*
but read a pamphlet in the Cave
  of the Apocalypse.

It was God — so the worthy archimandrite
(a natural poet, it seems, whose Englished prose
falls into almost pure iambic lines)
informs me — God who had guided me there —
Supreme Tour Operator, Master
of Ferry Schedules? — so that I might listen
deep within myself to the secret echo
of the words spoken to Saint John, so I
might see with my mind's eye the heavenly vision
  revealed to the Apostle.

The Apostle? Here already I part company
with our archimandrite ("Superior
of the Holy Cave of the Apocalypse")
and all his church, for on stylistic
grounds alone it's scarcely conceivable the author
of John's Gospel could have penned the Revelations.
"All styles are God's, my child," he might reply.
All styles and none — the elusive trademark
scratched on rock or scrawled in cloud across the sky,
the Rorshach islands of an enclosed sea . . .

I've seen the fissure in the rock from which
God spoke, dictating letters *to the seven*
churches which are, or were, the leaflet
seems to be suggesting, as recently
as nineteen-twenty-two, *in Asia* still,
"whose light, alas, has been extinguished
because their faith in God grew cold".
The archimandrite's subtext here
concerns the Turks — the politics
of the Apocalypse lives on! —
allowed like Satan's armies for a time
to wreak God's wrath upon the earth.

I've seen the fissure in the rock
and the small hollow in the cave wall, where,
we are expected to believe, Saint John,
when praying, used to rest his hands.
This little hole, glassed over now and framed
with an oval frame of embossed silver,
reminds me of a curious detail in one
of Gabriel García Márquez' stories: a woman,
newly married, finally presents herself,
after much procrastination, to her husband,
supine and wearing a white robe that covers her
from chin to toes, with one small opening,
no larger than was strictly necessary,
edged like a button hole, about a foot
below her waist. It was, her husband thought,
the most obscene thing he'd ever seen.

And why would any saint or sinner kneel
to pray pressed up against a wall, his hands
nestled inside a pocket in the rock about
waist-high; or, for that matter, lie to sleep,
his head inside another larger hole
four or five inches from the floor, protected now
by a fence of polished brass, so even the pious
imagination finds it difficult
to detect the holyman in his supposed repose.

A sloping shelf in the rock wall is draped
with rich brocades whose colours change (the evidence
of various cards and photographs in books) according
to the feast or season. This is the lectern
where Prochoros, Saint John's amanuensis,
stood to write. Odd that the older icons show him
seated and writing at a table or on his knees.
But then the archimandrite speaks about "the struggle
against Antichrist and his *tools*" . . .

. . . and I wonder if some monastic chisel might not
have once advanced God's handiwork in stone.

Sea voices

I have escaped to this island...
The sea is high again today...
At night when the wind roars...

Lawrence Durrell, *Justine*

I too have come to an island —
island in time, out of the flux
of time — carried by currents and tides,
as unchoosing as the cave
of the voices it shall echo.

When the sea is high, when the wind roars,
I have no peace, I cling to the rocks,
press my face to the cave's floor.

The sea has many voices,
     alluring voices.
I want to follow,
     but I cling . . .

And in the quiet nights,
the cave echoes my voice,
echoing those other voices
that have found a hold in me,
     and in me speak
their shattered phrases,
     endlessly.

The silence of the icons
("a periphrastic study in a worn-out poetical fashion")

When the icons no longer spoke to us
we sought out solitary old men in high places
where the wind bites into the brain.

Whole days we squatted on low stools,
warming our hands at a small fire
in the corner of a rough stone hut,
water seeping through the turf roof
and hardly a word spoken, straining
to read his meaning in the inclination
of his body, or the unmoving eyes,
where, from time to time in the dim light,
the flames danced.
                              And another we found,
gone almost blind at the back of a cave,
whose cracked laughter — hollow yet filled
with a kind of life too remote for envy —
greeted our every question.
                              Or the one
we never saw, who wouldn't move
from his bed behind the curtain of old
blankets that served to make two rooms
of that small house, who spoke only in harsh
grunts, complaining we were pestering him
like flies.
                              But *there* was a young woman also,
a granddaughter we supposed, who waited on him.
She was tall, strong-limbed, about eighteen,
and moved with such sure steps in that cramped space,

and when she offered us water we heard
it leap in her voice over sun-bleached stones,
and in her eyes laughter flickered like far-off
lightning. For hers were all those other seasons
that grim December house would never know.

And we knew then that we were wrong,
that whatever wisdom it was
these old men clutched so tightly to themselves
it was not for us who were still in the midst
of things; nor could we simply take
the light and laughter of the girl,
weighed down as we were already
by so many mistakes, and some, who might
have forgiven us, no longer alive.

Before we parted, we spoke together in our ponderous
fashion of finding some middle way
between the young woman — red petals still furled
about the dark centre of the poppy,
waiting on the sun's heat to spread those limbs —
and the old men — so far in love with death
that they had left the world early to spend
long years in her cold company,
taking strange pleasure in putting off so long
the moment when they would set aside their rags
to stretch their withered nakedness
along the length of her cold marble form
and have her draw from deep inside of them
the last few drops of human warmth.

Not untinged then with contempt the indifference

we have learned for those whom first we sought to teach us,
those who have let death slowly suck them dry,
whose withered husks litter the mind, refusing
to decay.
        But of her we would speak with care,
knowing how fragile such proud strength may prove,
remembering how our own brightness faltered
when we failed to grasp with both hands
what stood before us to be taken,
and the dead years that followed,
when more and more each went alone behind
closed doors with his own particular ghosts,
and every spring the blossoms on the almond
in the yard behind the house were fewer
than before, and one by one the mouths
of the once-living icons were stopped
until their silence hounded us
from room to room and rose inside us
like a scream that could never find the throat,
and we fled, looking for warmth in the mountains
in winter, for light in the depths of caves,
and the narrow stone-built roads we'd read of
in old books — long since obliterated
under the newer ways — and found instead
this one red flower, sprung out of season
among the stones.
        Once we had separated,
knowing there was no road we could tread together
any more, I went back alone
in the foolish hope of seeing her again,
but I found no smoke in the chimney,
the windows boarded and the door locked.

I sat instead for a long time
on the steep bank of a small lake
we had missed before, whose black mirror
vibrated to a silence so finely detailed
it seemed to hold all the sounds of the world,
but at infinite distance, and I felt
myself stretched, taut as the strings of a lute
now tuned to a new and unheard pattern
for which no music yet exists,
while, all around, white rocks
trembled in the light.

NOTES

On the scope of these notes and the reasons for their inclusion, see the Introduction, p. xvi. In each Note the title is preceded by the page number(s) of the poem concerned.

Memorials

6. Theatre of Dionysus, Athens
When I visited the ruins of this theatre sometime around 1990, restoration work was in progress and parts of columns and other architectural elements were indeed "laid out in rows" to one side of the stage area. Other details belong to the permanent state of this monument. In classical times competitive theatrical performances in the theatre were part of religious festivals. Each dramatist had to provide a trilogy of tragedies and a humorous satyr play. The *Oresteia* of Aeschylus, consisting of *Agamemnon, The libation bearers* and *The Eumenides*, is the only complete trilogy to have survived.

7–8. That afternoon
While the description of my grandfather, the details of the sitting room and of family visits to the house for Sunday tea are accurate, the subjective account of his death is (in part of necessity) imaginary. In reality he died in his sleep, and in November, not the implied summer of the poem.

9. Homecomings
This poem is an account of a scene that I observed in the 1990s in the harbour of Kamariotissa on the island of Samothraki. There is only a small element of speculation: I didn't know that the dead man was a farmer from an upland village, nor, of course, did I know what his wife was thinking as she emerged from the ship.

10. Greek mariners *or* The naming of craft
This poem arose out of a day when I travelled by ship from Piraeus to

Poros, and observed the names of the large car ferries at the harbour in Piraeus and the names of many of the small fishing boats tied up at the wharf in Poros, and was struck by the contrast between the two groups of names. The phrase "pre-apostolic trade" refers to the circumstance that a number of the twelve disciples (later known as apostles) were fishermen, recruited by Jesus on the shore of the Sea of Galilee (Matthew 4.18-22, also in Mark and Luke).

13. Coincidence (1st of October 1991)
The 1st of October 1991 was when the Siege of Dubrovnik began. Dubrovnik is a city of great antiquity and historical significance and an important port in Croatia. Croatia had recently declared its independence from the Federal Republic of Yugoslavia. The siege of the city was part of an ultimately unsuccessful attempt by Serbia and Montenegro to re-establish Federal control of Croatia. Dubrovnik was also shelled from the land by the Yugoslav People's Army, which had already taken control of most of the territory around the city. Blockade was the main function of the Federal Navy in the Siege. As for "the workplace", I was at the time working as a postman and had just "emerged" from the London E2 (Bethnal Green) sorting office, where Capital Radio was always playing all day long.

15. Poison on Poros
A *trivium* is a point at which three roads meet. A *temenos* is the enclosed sacred area around an ancient Greek temple, in this case one dedicated to the sea-god Poseidon. Demosthenes (384–322 BC) was an Athenian politician who championed Athens' resistance to the domination of Macedonia, a rising power, which, under its kings Phillip II, his son Alexander III (Alexander the Great) and Alexander's successor Antipater, came to control the entire Greek World. When the cause of Athenian independence was finally lost Demosthenes was condemned to death but escaped to the island of Kalaureia (now known as Poros). When he was discovered there, he chose to commit suicide by taking poison, rather than be arrested.

19. War dead
The village of Lemós (in Greek Λαιμός) is situated close to the lake of

Megáli Préspa, in the middle of which three borders meet, those of Greece, Albania and what is now called Northern Macedonia, still part of Yugoslavia at the time of my visit, and in the interim known as the Former Yugoslav Republic of Macedonia (or FYROM). This is one reason why I say that the nearby mountain pass was "no doubt contested more than once". I was urged to replace the words "died in hospitals" by the conventional English expression "died of wounds", but I decided to retain it, first because it accurately translates the Greek on the village war memorial, and secondly because, before the discovery of penicillin, many soldiers in field hospitals, and indeed in regular hospitals away from areas of conflict, died from infections unrelated to their wounds.

20. In Salonica today the sea
Leofóros Níkis means Avenue of Victory. The sun was "smeared black with smoke" because the forests on "the hills across the gulf" were on fire. Forest fires — natural, accidental or the result of arson — are common occurrences in Greece in the summer.

22. Still life, Sigh . . . gone
After the Reunification of Vietnam in 1975 Saigon was renamed Ho Chi Minh City.

23. In the Commonwealth Cemetry at Souda
Most of the dead from the Battle of Crete, May 1941, lie in the two large cemeteries in northwestern Crete referred to here. On the German dead, see also "Memorials (1941, 1989)".

25. The effects of Alcohol
I first encountered David Cooper, the briefly famous (some might prefer "notorious") author and self-styled "antipsychiatrist", at the Dialectics of Liberation Congress in London in 1967 (see below in the note to pp. 37–8). A few years later, through a mutual friend, I got to know him at a time when his personal life, professional work and alcoholism were all out of control and he was at times homeless. At one such period he lived in our house on and off for several weeks.

26. In memoriam L.G.D.

The initials are those of Lawrence George Durrell, but also of L. G. Darley, Durrell's first-person narrator in the novels *Justine*, *Balthazar* and *Clea* — the first, second and fourth parts of *The Alexandria Quartet*. Darley's forenames are never disclosed, but the character, Pursewarden, a novelist and diplomat, refers to him as "Lineaments", translating his initials into Blake's phrase "lineaments of gratified desire". This poem is something of a collage incorporating many words and phrases from *The Alexandria Quartet*. These are in italics in the relevant sections below, where page numbers in *Justine* (J) and *Balthazar* (B) are given in the right margin, together with the original words where a single word in a phrase has been replaced by another (underlined below) in the poem. Not all consecutive italicized words are consecutive in the original novels: words have been omitted here and there or the word or phrase order changed. Page references are to the first Faber editions of *Justine* (1956) and *Balthazar* (1958). Later editions, including the one-volume editions of the *Quartet*, are flawed by careless revisions, perhaps in response to reader's complaints about inconsistencies, especially as regards temporal sequence, in the original publications.

Durrell, living in the hills of Cyprus
with an infant daughter, writes as Darley,
escaped with a few books and the child —   J13
Melissa's child — *to heal <u>himself</u>* on some   /myself J13
unnamed *Aegean island* (*snatched*   B13, J13
<u>*each*</u> *night from darkness by Arcturus*)   /every J13
where *the Smyrna packet* en route   B17
from Alexandria's *delayed*   B19
one *Thursday* night with *engine trouble*   B17, B19
and deposits *on <u>his</u> doorstep* Balthazar,   /your B19
that fictional acquaintance of Cavafy
(*the old poet of the city*), clutching the *manuscript*   J14, B18
in which he has insinuated, *interlinear*,   B18
one construct's perceptions, constructed to correct
another construct's reconstructions
of lives that no one ever lived,
the product of *<u>returning</u> link by link*   /I return J13
along the iron chains of memory   J13
to <u>a</u> city inhabited so briefly . . .   /the J13

Only *the city* — and its poet — *wholly real.*	B13
[...]	
And Darley, technically immortal,	
will *be here, as always, <u>writing</u> by the water,*	/smoking J245
the night sky dusted thickly with stars.	J245

As for Lorca and "the music of those Braque guitars", I have done word searches for both "guitara(s)" and "Braque" in an online edition of the *Obras (Works)* of Federico Garcia Lorca without turning up the quotation. It seems that I took it from a secondary source, *The politics of experience* (penultimate paragraph of Chapter 1), by R. D. Laing: "Creation ex nihilo has been pronounced impossible even for God. But we are concerned with miracles. We must hear the music of those Braque guitars (Lorca)."

30. Anna Palaiologou's gate
In 1326 Anna, the daughter of the Count of Savoy, married the Byzantine Emperor Andronikos III Palaiologos, who was then involved in a civil war with his grandfather, Andronikos II. This ended with the victory of the grandson in 1328. When Andronikos III died in 1341, he was succeeded by their eight-year-old son John V. Anna was appointed regent, but soon became embroiled in another civil war with Andronikos' close associate John Kantakouzenos, who had been proclaimed emperor by the army. This conflict lasted until 1347 when Kantakouzenos, as John VI, became the senior emperor with the young John V as co-emperor. In 1351 Anna Palaiologou moved to Thessaloniki (Thessalonica) where she set up a semi-autonomous local administration.

33–36. Bashō, Oppenheimer, and a dream
(33) The sources of the epigraphs are as follows. Oppenheimer: *Lawrence and Oppenheimer* by Nuel Pharr Davis (New York: Simon & Schuster, 1968), p. 355; Bashō: *The Narrow Road to the Deep North and Other Travel Sketches*, translated from the Japanese by Nobuyuki Yuasa (Harmondsworth: Penguin Books, 1966), p. 51; T. S. Eliot: *Four Quartets*, "East Coker", V.
(34) On "sweet", the full quotation from Oppenheimer is: "When you see something that is technically sweet, you go ahead and do it and you

argue about what to do about it only after you have had your technical success. That is the way it was with the atomic bomb." Los Alamos was the headquarters of the Manhattan Project of the US Department of War, set up in 1943 with the prime objective of developing a nuclear bomb. Oppenheimer was the director of the laboratory at Los Alamos.

(35) The *Bhagavad Gita* is one of the key sacred books of Hinduism, a dialogue before a battle between Prince Arjuna and the supreme god Krishna in the guise of Arjuna's chariot driver. The quotation is from Chapter 10, verse 34, and a more literal translation is "I am Death, the destroyer of all". We have come to refer to the visible signs of a nuclear explosion in the atmosphere above the detonation as a "mushoom cloud" (the "great cloud rising" on p. 36); the "fruiting body" of mushrooms and other fungi is the part that contains the spores, which in mushrooms is the "cap", the part on the top of the stem. "Point Zero" was the test site in the Jornada del Muerto desert in New Miexico where the first nuclear test took place (of the type of bomb soon after dropped on Nagasaki). The "force to break, blow burn" comes from John Donne's Holy Sonnet 14 which begins "Batter my heart, three person'd God". As for "Twin stars of *our* birth", I was born in 1945 just a few months before the bombing of Hiroshma on the 6th of August and Nagasaki "a few days later" on the 9th. But, more generally, "*our* birth" because, like the mythical star that marked the birth of Jesus and the start of the Christian era, the explosion at Hiroshima can be seen as marking the start of a new era — conceivably a very short final era — in the sorry tale of human "civilization". Indeed, the "Publisher's Note" to the Penguin edition of John Hersey's *Hiroshima*, published in 1946, begins, "On Monday, August 6th, 1945, a new era in human history opened." "Little Boy" and "Fat Man" were the chillingly humorous names given, respectively, to the uranium bomb dropped on Hiroshima and the plutonium bomb ("a slightly altered score") dropped on Nagasaki, the latter name referring to the shape of the bomb, rather like a giant and over-inflated version of the balls used in rugby and American football.

(36) The "great cloud rising", as noted above, refers to the "mushroom cloud" of a nuclear explosion, but also alludes to a hymn by Charles Wesley: "Saw ye not the cloud arise / Little as a human hand? / Now it spreads along the skies, / Hangs o'er all the thirsty land". In the hymn, however, the cloud is benign: the shower that it promises is the outpouring of the Spirit of God's love. The phrases "a stain on a pavement" and "a shadow on a wall" refer to inhabitants of Hiroshima who were so close to centre of the explosion that their bodies were effectively vaporized by the extreme heat, leaving only silhouettes on adjacent surfaces.

(37) In April and May 1954 Oppenheimer had to appear before the House Un-American Activities Comittee to be "investigated" regarding his former associations with members of the Communist Party and his alleged communist sympathies. As a result he was stripped of his security clearance and thus debarred from working on scientific research projects for the U.S. government. So he "returned to teaching", writing, public lecturing, and campaigning internationally for scientific independence from government control.

(37–8) Gregory Bateson reported Oppenheimer's words at the Dialectics of Liberation Congress (which I attended) at the Round House, Chalk Farm, London, in July 1967. Quietism ("now the Quietist") is a form of Christianity that arose in the late 18th century advocating the emptying of the mind over verbal prayer, and passive contemplation over supposedly well-intentioned intervention in the affairs of the world. It was condemned by both Catholics and Protestants.

39–41. Memorials (1941, 1989)

(39) The opening quotation is from p. 257 of the 1988 edition of *Blue Guide Crete*. *Fallschirmjägern* is the German equivalent of "paratroopers": *Fall-schirm* = fall + umbrella; Jägern = hunters. The normal plural would now be *Fallschirmjäger*, not different from the singular, but final N is present in the inscription referrred to. The town of "the town's westward sprawl" is Chania, which in 1941 was still the capital of Crete.

(41) "Bitter fruit" was a 1937 poem by Lewis Allan, the pen-name of Abel Meerpol (1903–1986), an American schoolteacher of Russian–Jewish origin. Made famous by Billie Holiday as a song, with the title "Strange fruit", it concerns the lynching from trees of Black Americans by unauthorized white lynch mobs: "Black bodies swinging in the southern breeze / strange fruit hanging from the poplar trees". The expression "all ye that pass by" alludes to a biblical lament over the destruction of Jerusalem, where Jerusalem herself speaks: "Is it nothing to you, all ye that pass by? behold and see if there be any sorrow like unto my sorrow" (Lamentations 1.12). Christians have sometimes interpreted this as though it were Jesus speaking from the Cross.

42–45. Ka and Kavafis

Orhan Pamuk, awarded the Nobel Prize in Literature in 2006, is a Turkish novelist and a controversial figure in his own country. His seventh novel *Snow* was published in 2002, the English translation following in 2004. C. P. Cavafy (or K. P. Kavafis in Greek, 1863–1933) is the best known and most widely translated of Modern Greek poets, though his reputation rests on 154 mainly short poems. His *Ateli piimata* (*Unfinished Poems*) were not published until 1994. Yuri Zhivago, a doctor and a poet, is the principal character in the Russian novel *Doctor Zhivago* by Boris Pasternak (1890–1960). Refused publication in Russia, it was first published in Italy in 1957 in Italian translation, quickly followed by translations into many other languages. Pasternak was awarded the Nobel Prize in Literature in 1958 largely on the basis of *Doctor Zhivago*, but the Soviet government prevented him from receiving it. The poems of his fictional character are printed at the end of the novel.

46–49. The family plot, Salendine Nook Baptist Cemetery

(46) Salendine Nook is a district on the western edge of Huddersfield, Yorkshire. The cemetery is next to the "main Rochdale Road" (see "Here's to you, Ma" on p. 37), which was, before the construction of the M6 Motorway one of the principal routes over the Pennine moors into Lancashire. "C of E" = Church of England.

(47) "the football people and the lawyers": my grandfather (born 1878) was one of the founders of Huddersfield Town Football Club and was Chairman of the U.K. Football Association from 1941 until shortly before his death in 1955. In his professional career he started as a solicitor and became a County Court Registrar.

(49) When she read this poem many years ago, my sister said that no way would she be buried there. So the last remaining space in the family plot is mine should I want it.

Nightscapes, seascapes, lovescapes, landscapes . . .

53. Night conceits

I don't think that the italicized lines in archaic English in the first and last stanzas, are actual quotations, but, rather, that they just came to me in this form. The first one bears some resemblance to a line from a hymn by Ray Palmer, "Come, Jesus, from thy sapphire throne" (1876) in which the final verse (verse 6) begins "Come, faithful Shepherd, feed Thy sheep; / In Thine own arms the lambs enfold"; but I am not sure I ever came across this in my hymn-singing days. As for the second, the expressions "the river between us" and "the river runs between us" occur in a number of literary contexts.

54. Attic power cut

The epigraph, from Euripides' *Electra* (line 867), is partially translated in line 5 of the poem. The literal meaning of this paradoxical line is "O Earth and Night [*or* Darkness] which hitherto I clearly saw" and is uttered by Electra in a moment of triumph when she learns that her stepfather has been killed (the "slaughter") by her brother to avenge their father's death, and all is now light for her.

55. Lunch on Poros

"Helenic blue" refers to the light blue of the cross and the horizontal bands on a white background of the Greek flag — a colour combination which is also very common in the painting of traditional Greek houses: whitewashed walls and blue doors and windows.

57. "I do not think that they will sing to me"

The title is from T. S. Eliot's "The Love Song of J. Alfred Prufrock", where it is preceded by the line: "I have heard the mermaids singing each to each." On Masha, see Chekhov, *The Seagull*, the opening of Act I, where, asked why she always wears mourning, Masha replies that she dresses in black to suit her life because she is unhappy. Some English translations of the play have reversed the terms of the question and answer, such that in reply to the question "Why do you always wear black?" she says "I am in mourning for my life"; it is near the beginning of Act II that she refers to her life as "an endless train" and then says, in relation to her unhappiness, "I must shake myself and throw it off"; early in Act III she says "I just made up my mind [...] that I would tear this love out of my heart", and then "when I marry there will be no time left for love" (quotations here from *Four great plays by Chekhov*, translator unnamed, Bantam Classics, 1958).

60–61. Aegean snapshots 7 x 5

The "snapshot" beginning "Breaking the surface / of the antique / (Socratic) frog pond" imitates Bashō's famous haiku:

> Breaking the silence
> of an ancient pond,
> a frog jumped into the water —
> a deep resonance.

This translation is by Nobuyuki Yuasa, in Bashō, *The Narrow Road to the Deep North and Other Travel Sketches* (Harmondsworth: Penguin Books, 1966), p. 9. At the same time this "snapshot" alludes to Socrates' statement in Plato's *Phaedo* (109b) that the Greeks live around the Mediterranean like "frogs round a pond".

65. Volcano days

In the Apocalypse of John (as it is known in Greek) or the Book of Revelation, the writer describes a vision in which four horsemen appear in succession each on a horse of a different colour (white, red, black and pale), commonly referred to as the "four horsemen of the Apocalypse". Their role is to bring war and destruction to the earth as agents of God's wrath (Revelation 6.1–8, and see further the note to p. 204 below). In another vision the author says "I saw a woman sit upon a beast [...] having seven heads and ten horns. And the woman was arrayed in purple and scarlet colour, and gold and precious stones [...] and on her forehead was a name written, MYSTERY, BABYLON THE GREAT, THE MOTHER OF HARLOTS" (Revelation 17. 3–5); this figure is commonly referred to as "the Whore of Babylon". The idea of "Aphrodite's blind and blood-soaked smile" was generated by several expressions in Lawrence Durrell's *The Alexandria Quartet*: "austere and merciless Aphrodite" (J105), "the austere mindless primitive face of Aphrodite" (J109), "the divine trespass of an immortal among mortals

— Aphrodite-in-arms" (J197), "the cataract with which Aphrodite seals up the sick eyes of lovers, the thick, opaque form of a sacred sightlessness" (B54): page numbers in the first editions of *Justine* (J) and *Balthazar* (B).

66. Visitors
The "philosopher" is Swami Vivekananda (1863–1902) and the "Tamil poet" is the largely legendary Thiruvalluvar, thought to have lived at some time between the 4th century BC and the 6th century AD (but probably in the early part of that period), the author of the surviving religious/philosophical poem on the art of living known as *Tirukkural*. Disputes about the date of the author focus on analysis of the language of his poem.

70. Cloudscapes
Mount Ida is the highest mountain in Crete, situated towards the western end of the island.

73–74. The railway station in Kampala
I visited Uganda in 2008 when my younger daughter was living there. For other poems arising from that visit, see pp. 107–110.

84. Minoan royal prerogative
The location "where the road rises, steep, towards the palace" is the wide, stone-paved "Royal Road" which approaches the lower side of the site of the Minoan Palace of Knossos (Crete) from the northwest.

86. Tomb of Antipatros, a Macedonian
The phrase "valiants of pleasure" is, if the pluralization of the adjective "valiant" be allowed, a possible translation of the phrase *andreíoi tis idonís* in Cavafy's poem "I went": "I did not restrain myself. I let go completely and I went [...] in the brightly illuminated night. And I drank strong wines, such as the valiants of pleasure drink."

87. An die ferne Geliebte
The German title, meaning "To the distant beloved", is that of a song cycle by Beethoven. The lyrics of the six constituent songs by Alois

Isidore Jeitteles may have been written at Beethoven's request. In the opening song the singer (a man) is sitting on a hilltop peering through the blue haze towards the distant place where he first met the woman to whom the songs are addressed.

88. Anticipating spring

The names Venus (Latin) and Aphrodite (Greek) are interchangeable names for the goddess of love; and the planet we call Venus is known in Greek as Aphrodite. Though the etymology of Aphrodite is uncertain it has generally been taken, following Hesiod, to mean "risen from the foam", that is, the foam of the sea. In one of the Greek myths, the Titan Kronos cut off the genitals of his father Ouranos (Uranus), the sky god, and threw them into the sea where they generated foam from which Aphrodite emerged.

89. Sleeping, not leaping

The poet Sappho was said by some ancient authors to have killed herself by jumping from a cliff when her love for a ferryman was not returned. Cape Lefkas on the Ionian island of Lefkada is known as Sappho's Leap, though it is an improbably long way from Sappho's home in Mytilene (Lesvos) on the eastern side of the Aegean. The woman to whom this poem and the previous two are addressed lived for many years with cancer before taking advantage of Oregon's law permitting medically assisted dying to make her dignified exit from the world (one form of her "contingency plans").

90. Travelling alone

The "Seferis poem" in question is Μὲ τὸν τρόπο τοῦ Γ. Σ., "In the manner of G. S.", the initials presumably standing for George Seferis, and thus suggesting self parody. Its first line means "Wherever I travel Greece wounds me".

91. These places

The location of "these places" is Crete, though much of the detail could equally derive from other parts of Greece; "where Europe began": because European culture is often considered to have begun with the Minoan civilization of Crete; "where Europe ends" because

Crete, or more precisely a small island off its south coast is, the southernmost part of Europe. The poem dates from 1988.

92. TV in Vietnam in 2012
In the last stanza "the crafty mouse" and "the greedy cat" may be read as referring to the differing military strategies and strengths of the Viet Cong and the U.S. forces in the Vietnam War.

96. Plateia Varnava, Athens
Saint Paul saw marriage as an inferior state, of value only as a defence against sin: "It is good for a man not to touch a woman. Nevertheless to avoid fornication, let very man have his own wife and let every woman have her own husband [...] I would that all men were even as I myself [i.e. celibate]. I say [...] to the unmarried and widows, It is good for them if they abide even as I. But if they cannot contain [their desires], let them marry: for it is better to marry than to burn" (I Corinthians 7, 1–2 and 7–9). Saint Barnabas accompanied Paul on his early missionary journeys. I describe Paul as an "erratic moralist" both in relation to his extensive travels ("erratic" as "wandering") and also because of the improvisatory feel of, and inconsistencies in, his off-the-cuff invention of Christian doctrine and moral principles in the course of his rambling epistles ("erratic" as "irregular in behaviour").

99. The swallows of Kastoriá
Kastoriá is a lakeside city in northern Greece in the administrative region of Western Macedonia.

101. The quick and the dead
"Quick" is used in its archaic meaning of "alive" or "living". The phrase "the quick and the dead" is of biblical origin: "I charge you therefore before God and the Lord Jesus Christ who shall judge the quick and the dead at his appearing in his kingdom" (II Timothy 4.1), but is perhaps better known from its adoption in the translations of the Nicene and Apostles' Creeds in the Anglican *Book of Common Prayer*.

103. . . . and I, I lie alone
The title is the ending of a well-known poem attributed to Sappho,

which I give here in my own translation:

> The moon has set,
> the Pleiades as well,
> it is the middle of the night,
> the watch is going by,
> and I, I lie alone.

104–105. London winter evening: linked verse

(104) "Linked verse" is a Japanese practice going back to the fourteenth century, in which a number of poets sitting together compose verses in succession, each verse responding in some way to the preceding one.

(105) In the Greek myth of Theseus and the Minotaur, Ariadne is the daughter of King Minos of Crete. Crete was plagued by the Minotaur, (half man, half bull) who lived in a Labyrinth. When Theseus, a prince of Athens, undertook to confront the Minotaur, Ariadne gave him a ball of thread: unwinding it as he entered the Labyrinth, he would be able to find his way out if he was not killed by the Minotaur. Theseus killed the Minotaur and as promised took Ariadne away with him but abandoned her on the island of Naxos on his way back to Athens. The lines "beside the gate / with golden string" allude to William Blake, *Jerusalem* IV.77 (which may in turn allude to Ariadne's thread):

> I give you the end of a golden string,
>   Only wind it into a ball,
> It will lead you in at Heaven's gate
>   Built in Jerusalem's wall.

106. The journey to Asine

Asine (pronounced *A-see-nee*) is a small coastal resort in the Peloponnese beside the site of ancient city of the same name. The surviving architectural remains on the rocky citadel are very limited. The italicized elements in the poem translate phrases from George Seferis' poem "The King of Asine". In the "catalogue of ships" in Homer's *Iliad*, Asine is mentioned as one of the kingdoms (really tribal fiefdoms) which contributed ships to the Achaean (Greek) fleet that sailed to Troy in support of Menelaus, King of Mycenae, whose wife Helen ("Helen of Troy") had been abducted by the Trojan prince, Paris. From the single phrase in Homer, *Asinên te* ("and Asine") Seferis attempts to conjure up the ancient King of Asine of whom nothing else at all is known.

108. Mahoma Falls
The Falls are located in the Crater Lakes area of western Uganda (see the next poem).

110. Capitals
Kampala is not far from the Great Rift Valley, which is sometimes referred to as the "Cradle of Mankind", because there some of the earliest evidence of our human ancestors has been found.

114–121. The Pilgrim's Way
The Pilgrim's Way is a modern approximation to the medieval pilgrim route stretching from Winchester in Hampshire to the shrine of Thomas Becket in Canterbury, Kent.

(117) The quotation from Ernest Hemingway in the middle poem on this page is spoken by a character in his novel of the Spanish Civil War *For whom the bell tolls* (chapter 43).

(118) "Church (rems of)" in the first poem on this page is an expression found frequently on Ordnance Survey maps of the UK (rems of = remains of). The "pilgrims" envisaged in the second poem on this page are those of Chaucer's *Canterbury Tales* (late 14th century).

'twixt earnest and joke

All of the uncredited epigraphs to these poems are from the Song of Solomon (elsewhere known as the Song of Songs) as it appears in the Authorized (King James) Version of the Bible of 1611. I make no apology for attaching these verses from "Holy Scripture" to my half-humorous erotic poems. The theological interpretations of the Song of Songs as an allegory — in Judaism of the love between God and his people; in Christianity of the love between Christ and his "bride" the Church — are equally and patently absurd. There is not a hint of religion in it anywhere. Part narrative soliloquy, part dialogue with chorus, it is simply one of the most marvelous love poems to have reached us from the ancient world — perhaps *the* most marvelous. We should acknowledge, though, that it is largely due to its religious misinterpretations that it has reached us at all. It is obscure in places and has no doubt suffered in transmission through scribal errors, and perhaps been subject to some rearrangement of its parts — it has even been suggested that it is a collection of poems. Its association with, and authorship by, the proverbially wise King Solomon have often been questioned; and the seven occurrences of his name in the text (with or without the prefix "king") may have been inserted after its original composition to give it greater authority as a religious allegory. They occur at the beginning (1.1 and 1.5) and end (8.11, 8.12) with a group of three close together in the middle at 3.7, 3.9 and 3.11.

The chapter-and-verse references for the epigraphs — in which I have frequently changed the gender or person of the pronouns and possessives — are set out in the following table.

Page No	Opening words	Chapter and verse
127	Thy lips are like a thread of scarlet	4.3
128	Thou hast ravished my heart	4.9
129	Turn away thine eyes from me	6.5
130	Let her kiss me with the kisses of her mouth	1.2
131	Thy lips , O my spouse	4.11
132	Her hands are as gold rings set with beryl	5.14
135	O my dove, that art in the clefts of the rock	2.14
137	By night on my bed I sought her	3.1
139	Who is she that looketh forth as the morning	6.10
141	Many waters cannot quench love	8.7
142	Who is this that cometh out of the wilderness	3.6
143	I sleep, but my heart waketh	5.2
144	My beloved put in her hand	5.4
146	I charge you, O ye daughters of Jerusalem	2.7
147	I opened to my beloved	5.6
149	She brought me to the banqueting house	2.4
150	My beloved spake, and said unto me	2.10
151	There are threescore queens	6.8

155	Thy cheeks are comely with rows of jewels	1.10–11
156	Eat, O friends; drink	5.1
157	Set me as a seal upon thine heart	8.6
158	Behold thou art fair, my beloved	1.16–17
159	A fountain of gardens	4.15–16
162	Until the day break	4.6
163	Who is this that cometh up	8.5
164	I called her but she gave me no answer	5.6
166	The keepers of the walls	5.7

126. ἅλς ἰόνιος / hals ionios (Ionian Sea)

The Greek poet C. P. Cavafy lived most of his life in Alexandria, Egypt, apart from a few years in England in his childhood and a period in Istanbul in his late teenage years. He never lived in Greece, but made a number of visits. One of these took place in 1901, in the company of Alexander, one of his older brothers. They left Alexandria on the 13th of June and arrived back on the 5th of August, having spent most of their time in Athens, but making the return journey via Corfu and the Italian port of Brindisi. Throughout this trip he kept a diary, in English. On the 1st of August he writes, "Yesterday afternoon A. and I left Patras on board the Rubatino Steamship 'Scilla'. [...] The site of Patras with its many lights slowly fading away was very pretty." And on the 4th of August he continues, "We reached Corfu early in the morning on the 1st August. Alexander and I went ashore at 9. [...] We returned to the ship at 2 p.m. [...] We sailed at 5 p.m. [...] At 3 a.m. we reached Brindisi. [...] All the passengers left the 'Scilla' at 8 a.m.; but we were on and off her until 1 p.m. when the Austrian S.S. 'Bohemia' arrived. We transported our luggage from the 'Scilla' to the 'Bohemia'. [...] Yesterday (the 3d Augsut) I passed quite agreeably on the 'Bohemia'. The weather is excellent and the food perfect. The 'Bohemia' left Brindisi at 3 p.m. the day before yesterday (2d August). [...] Yesterday at about 10 a.m. we saw the coast of Corfu." These sparse and banal details are the only record the diary offers of the time — the only time — that Cavafy spent aboard ship in the Ionian Sea: first between Patras on the Greek mainland and the island of Corfu; then between Corfu and Brindisi; finally on the first stage of the return voyage to Alexandria. To which of those three periods at sea the poem "Of the ship" belongs it is not possible to say with certainty, but I suspect it was the last, on the 3rd of August when he passed the day "quite agreeably" in "excellent" weather; he complains of cramped conditions on the *Scilla*, which he describes as "a wretched ship", compared with the *Bohemia* which he finds "a splendid ship". The poem was written in October 1919, more than eighteen years after Cavafy's passages through the Ionian Sea, and first published three months after that date. Here is the whole of the poem in my translation:

It's like him, certainly, this little
portrait of him in pencil.

Hastily done, on the deck of the ship;
one marvellous afternoon.
The Ionian Sea all around us.

It's like him. Though I recall him being more beautiful.
He was an aesthete to the point of suffering,
and this illuminated his expression.
More beautiful he seems to me
now that my mind has called him back from Time.

From Time. These things are all so very old —
the sketch, the ship, the afternoon.

The diary offers two potential candidates for the young aesthete of the sketch, in addition to Cavafy's brother Alexander. Writing, again on the 4th of August, after the reference to the *Bohemia* sailing from Brindisi on the 2nd of August, he notes "There are very few first class passengers on board, of which only one acquaintance of mine, Blattner, of Lambert & Ralli. The only other passengers whose names I've learned is [*sic*] a Mme Axisa and her son." But there may have been no actual sketch which the poet still possessed all those years later; the whole poem may be a fantasy arising from the distant memory of an agreeable day at sea. As for Cavafy having "marked the spot" of my poem it would have been on the second stage, from Corfu to Brindisi, that he sailed northward up the eastern coast of Corfu, and through the narrow Corfu Channel which separates the northern part of the island from Albania (then simply a part of the Ottoman Empire); this is also the route to Sarandë (see the following note).

127. As on lips I fixed my gaze
Sycorax, the mother of Caliban, is an off-stage character in Shakespeare's *The Tempest*. Count D, a real person in Lawrence Durrell's semi-fictional *Prospero's Cell: A guide to the landscape and manners of the island of Corcyra* (the ancient name for Corfu), argues that Corfu must have been the intended location of Shakespeare's play (pp. 78–80). That Durrell agreed is evident from his calling the book *Prospero's Cell* after one of the principal characters in the play. "Forty Saints" translates the Greek name *Ayi Saranda* of the Albanian port, known in Albanian as Sarandë, from which we travelled by coach to Butrint. The "Forty Saints" were the Forty Martyrs of Sebaste (now Sivas in Turkey), who, during the persecution of Christians in the early 4th century, were placed naked, under guard, on a frozen lake to die of cold.

132. So nail your courage to the sticking-place
"Lady Macbeth misquoted" because what she actually says to her husband in Shakespeare's play, as they plan the murder of King Duncan, is "*But screw* your courage to the sticking-place, / And we'll not fail*" (*Macbeth*, Act 1, Scene 7). Robert Browning (1812–1889) is invoked because I fancied some affinity with the style of his more casual unrhymed dramatic monologues, such as "Bishop Blougram's apology" (the bishop taking to task his critic) or "Andrea del Sarto" (the painter talking to his wife). Browning was, I think, the first English poet since Shakespeare to succeed (over hundreds of pages) in putting something very close to natural contemporary speech into verse, eschewing for the most part the archaic diction which had been — and remained well into the twentieth century — the staple of English poetry. The "displaced Venetian Square" is a small square in the old part of Cofu Town, where the Venetian Well and a restaurant of the same name are located. The "Esplanade" or Spianada is the social focal point of the town. Fayoum portraits are strikingly realistic painted images of individual dead Egyptians dating from the late 1st century BC onwards. They were originally incorporated into the cloths in which the dead bodies (mummies) were wrapped, positioned over their real faces. Most but not all of them were found at the necropolis of Fayoum.

135. Λάϊνος / Laïnos (Made of marble)

The "sombre poet of drowned love and the brief moment of self-knowledge before death" refers to two of the finest and most complete poems of Dionysios Solomos, originally from Zakinthos, who spent the latter part of his life in Corfu. In "The Cretan" a man and his fiancée, fleeing from Crete after the unsuccessful uprising against the Turks in the context of the Greek War of Independence, have been shipwrecked. The man (the speaker of the poem) is supporting the woman in the water and swimming with her. When he finally brings her to the shore he discovers she is dead ("drowned love"). In "The shark" Solomos imagines the experience of an actual British soldier who was killed by a shark while swimming off Corfu, and attributes to him a moment of self-realization immediately preceding his brutal death.

138. Σα λιόντισσα, σα λιοντάρι / Sa liondissa, sa liondari (Like a lioness, like a lion)

This intentionally naive Greek poem is written in rhyming couplets and in the 15-syllable iambic meter of many Greek folk songs, each line divided by at least a minor sense break after the eighth syllable. The switch from past tense to present is not unusual in Greek narration. Noah's Ark has become a kind of nursery story. The details may be found near the beginning of the Bible in the Book of Genesis (chapters 6–8), and similar stories from the ancient world are found in other cultural contexts. In Genesis, God observes the prevalence of wickedness in the world he has created and determines to destroy all life, "but Noah found grace in the eyes of the Lord", and the plan was changed. Noah and his family would be saved. God instructs Noah to build "an ark of gopher wood". The overall dimensions are specified and it has to have three levels of rooms inside. "And of every living thing of all flesh, two of every sort shalt thou bring into the ark, to keep them alive with thee; they shall be male and female." This done, God causes it "to rain forty days and forty nights" and the flood waters rise until all of the mountains are covered, and all living things not in the ark are destroyed. Eventually the flood waters begin to recede and the ark comes to rest "upon the mountains of Ararat". To find out if the land is dry yet, Noah sends out a female dove, three times at seven-day intervals. The first time she returns having "found no rest for the sole of her foot"; the second time, when she returns, "in her mouth was an olive leaf pluckt off"; and the third time she "returned not again unto him any more". And then Noah and his family and all the living things emerged from the ark to repopulate the earth.

139. Η Ἄλισον της Τροίας / I Álison tis Trías (Alison of Troy)
This poem borrows details from the Homeric account of the Trojan War, the *Iliad*. Helen of Troy, the wife of King Menelaus of Mycenae was abducted by the Trojan Prince Paris and taken to Troy. An Achaean (Greek) fleet of a thousand ships sailed from Greece to lay siege to Troy and reclaim Helen (sometimes referred to as "the face that launched a thousand ships"). The siege lasted twelve years. To stand on the ramparts of Troy would at times have put one in danger of being struck by "Achaean arrows". The Lagan is the river which flows through Belfast to the sea in Belfast Lough.

140. Also in sleep
The epigraph, from George Seferis' poem refers to Juan Visconti who, in the 14th century, had unwisely written to King Peter I of Cyprus (then in France) to inform him (falsely it was later determined) of the Queen's supposed infidelity (the king himself was openly adulterous).

151–154. Ναι, σ' όλο τον κόσμο σε γυρεύω / Nai, s'ólo ton kósmo se yirévo (Yes, through all the world I seek for you)
Liá is a mountain village in Epirus, on the Greek mainland roughly opposite Corfu. We went there in large coach party at the invitation of Nicholas Gage, author of *Eleni* (1983), the story of his mother's life. Gage was born and spent his early childhood in Liá and it was there that Eleni was executed in 1947 by communist forces during the Greek Civil War, for organizing the escape of her own children. Gage and his sisters reached America where their father had gone to work some years before. With the money from his writings, especially *Eleni*, Gage has funded much of the restoration work in the village in recent decades.

156. Alison + I
In lines 4–5 there is an allusion to a novel in the form of letters, *Les*

liaisons dangeureuses (1782), by Pierre Choderlos de Laclos. It concerns two aristocrats, one male one female, and their seduction, manipulation and explotiation of other people. They advise each other on techniques of seduction. Whether the novel is immoral or amoral is a matter of debate. The familiar expression "Eat, drink and be merry for tomorrow we die" is biblical in origin, though it doesn't occur in exactly this form anywhere in the Bible, since it combines two separate verses. At Ecclesiastes 8.15 we find "a man hath no better thing under the sun than to eat, and to drink, and to be merry", and at Isaiah 22.13 "let us eat and drink; for tomorrow we shall die", repeated at I Corinthians 15.32 with a change of tense: "we die".

157. Ars is longa, vita's brevis
The title is a bastardization of the well known Latin tag, "Ars longa, vita brevis" (Art long, life brief), originally from the Greek of the physician Hippocrates. The italicized words at the end translate the final words of Dante's *Divine Comedy*: "l'amor che move il sole e l'altre stelle", referring there to divine love.

159–160. In a solitary deck chair
"Bashō" refers to my copy of the Japanese poet's *The Narrow Road to the Deep North* (see the note to p. 33 or pp. 60–61). G 'n' T = gin and tonic. "The Tree of Idleness" is the title of a poem by Lawrence Durrell, and also of the collection of poems that contains it. In a note to the poem, Durrell explains the title as "the name of a tree which stands outside Bellapaix Abbey in Cyprus and which confers the gift of pure idleness on all who sit under it".

166. Lady Julian's offering
Lady Julian of Norwich (1342–*c.*1416) was a mystic and recluse who at the age of thirty, when she was seriously ill and was expected to die, had a series of visions of the sufferings of Christ, which became the core of her *Revelations of Divine Love*; she then recovered from her sickness. The expression "the road, not to Damascus, but Butrint" refers to the conversion of Saul of Tarsus, later known as Saint Paul. Saul was on his way to Damascus to continue his pursuit and arrest of Christians in the early years following the execution of Jesus. As he

approached Damascus he was struck down and blinded by a light and heard "a voice saying unto him, Saul, Saul why persecutest thou me? And he said, Who art thou, Lord? And the Lord said, I am Jesus whom thou persecutest" (Acts 9.3–5). Saul/Paul's belief in his confrontation with Jesus may well have been the original germ of the stories of Jesus' resurrection from the dead. The words "scales fell from my eyes" are borrowed from the aftermath of Saul's vision. The blinded man was led into Damascus where a Christian named Ananias went to him, as he had been instructed by "the Lord in a vision", and laid his hands on him "And immediately there fell from his eyes as it had been scales and he received his sight forthwith" (Acts 9.8–18).

Remnants of religion

169. The hands of God
On "Pantocrator" see the note to p. 177 below. The expression "pitches its intrusive tent in us" derives from John 1.14 (referring to birth of Christ): "And the word became flesh and dwelt among us", where "dwelt" represents the Greek verb *eskênôsen*, whose basic meaning is "pitched a tent"; it is related to the noun *skênê* originally meaning "tent", later applied to any dwelling.

170. A mixed blessing
The title, while it is a common English idiom for something which has both advantages and disadvantages, also invokes Gabriel's salutation to Mary at the Annunciation, "Hail, thou that art highly favoured, the Lord is with thee: blessed art thou among women" (Luke 1.28, and of course in the "Hail Mary"), and also Mary's words to her cousin Elizabeth (at the end of the "Magnificat"), "and behold all generations shall call me blessed" (Luke 1.48). "Overshadowing power" invokes Gabriel's explanation to Mary of how she might "conceive in [her] womb and bring forth a son", after she has said, "I know not a man": "the Holy Ghost shall come upon thee, and the power of the Highest shall overshadow thee" (Luke 1.31–35). The second stanza alludes to the Greek god Zeus who took the form of a swan to seduce Leda; and

the third to Zeus' impregnating Danaë in the form of a golden rain. Jacob's wrestling with an angel derives from Genesis 32.22–32 where his opponent is described as a man, though Jacob afterwards says "I have seen God face to face". The idea that his struggle was with an angel derives from Hosea 12.4, and this ambiguity is taken up in the third stanza: "God become angel". The italicized line in the fifth stanza comes from Simeon's words to Mary when Jesus was presented in the Temple forty days after his birth (Luke 2.35), while the last line alludes to the conclusion of a later incident: when Jesus was twelve his family visited Jerusalem at Passover and discovered only after a day's journey homeward that he was not "in the company"; returning to Jerusalem they found him, after three days, in the temple conversing with "the doctors"; when rebuked by Mary for the anxiety he had caused her and his "father" (i.e. Joseph), Jesus replied "wist ye not that I must be about my Father's business?" — where "Father" is presumably to be understood as referring to God; Jesus returned with them to Nazareth, "but his mother kept all these sayings in her heart" (Luke 2.41–51).

171–172. Klafthmonos Square, Athens, 25th of March 2001
The Gospel Riots began on the 5th of November 1901 when students from the Theology department of the University of Athens stormed the offices of the newspaper *Akropolis* in protest against the translation of the Gospel of Matthew into modern spoken Greek ("demotic") which it had published. More and more people joined the students and by the 8th of November (the Feast of the Archangels Michael and Gabriel) the number of the protesters in the centre of Athens had reached at least 20,000, perhaps as high as 50,000; and of the eight dead not one was a student. On the Massacre of the Innocents see the note to p. 173 below.

172. Visitation
The first part derives from the account of Mary's visit to her cousin Elizabeth, the mother of John the Baptist (the "Visitation"), Elizabeth being in the sixth month of her pregnancy (Luke, 1.39–45): "And it came to pass, that, when Elizabeth heard the salutation of Mary, the babe leaped in her womb" (verse 41). The expression "before whom he'd have to run" refers to John the Baptist's Greek epithet *Prodromos*

meaning "Forerunner" (of the Messiah, i.e. Jesus). The "other woman in his life" is Salome, who asked for the head of the imprisoned John the Baptist, as a reward for her dancing, which had pleased King Herod, her step-father (Mark 6.21–8, Matthew 14.6–11). In modern elaborations (distortions) of the biblical accounts, and especially Oscar Wilde's play *Salome*, her request is presented as revenge for John's indifference to her sexual advances when she had visited him in Herod's prison. The final phrase can be found in Jesus' words to his disciples in the Garden of Gethsemane shortly before his arrest: "My soul is exceeding sorrowful, even unto death" (Matthew 26.38).

173–175. Strange land: a child's story

(173) In the background of this "story" are the Massacre of the Innocents and the Flight into Egypt from the second chapter of the Gospel of Matthew, but the voice in the poem is not intended to be that of Jesus. "When Jesus was born in Bethlehem, behold there came wise men from the east to Jerusalem, saying Where is he that is born King of the Jews? for we have seen his star in the east, and are come to worship him. When Herod [the King of Judea] heard these things, he was troubled [...] And when he had gathered all the chief priests and scribes of the people together, he demanded of them where Christ should be born." The "chief priests and scribes" have become in the poem "magic mirrors", a motif in several fairy tales, such as "Snow White". The answer to Herod's question is "Bethlehem" and the wise men went there and "saw the young child with Mary his mother". Herod had told them to "bring [him] word" when they had found the child, but they were "warned of God in a dream that they should not return to Herod" and "departed into their own country". At this time Joseph, the husband of Mary, was told by an angel in a dream, "take the young child and his mother and flee into Egypt [...] for Herod will seek the young child to destroy him." And sure enough, "Herod, when he saw that he was mocked of the wise men, was exceeding wroth [compare 'maddened kings'] and sent forth and slew [compare 'they sharpened their knives'] all the children in Bethlehm, and in all the coasts thereof, from two years old and under" (Matthew 2.1–16) — this is the Massacre of the Innocents. The second paragraph alludes to the "tree of the knowledge of good and evil" in the Garden of Eden — the only tree from which Adam (before the creation of Eve) was forbidden by God to eat. Later "the serpent" provoked Eve to disobey God's command "and she took of the fruit thereof, and did eat, and gave also to her husband with her; and he did eat. And the eyes of both of them were opened" (Genesis 3.1–7). The "you" of the poem is a grown-up version of a girl I knew only in a recurrent dream of my childhood. She was two or three years older than me. In the dream we were always walking together along a dirt road, very like the undeveloped part of my childhood street, which remained a track between two fields for about twenty years after house construction was halted by the Second World War. It was a wordless relationship, but her presence gave me strength. I knew that she understood all the things that I didn't. And her understanding was enough. The admittedly absurd idea of God as "a clown on a bicycle" also comes from my childhood, but earlier. Among my toys was a metal figure of a clown about 4cm tall. The clown-suit was white with red spots, the trousers baggy at the thighs, tight at the ankles; a matching conical hat had a red pompom on the top. There was also a white bicycle with wheels that revolved and the clown's legs were separated so that he could be placed astride the bicycle. My (I guess) four-year-old mind took this clown to be an representation of God, about whom, before I went to school, I had heard very little; and I regarded it with a kind of primitive awe. Sometimes I was afraid to open the door of the sideboard cupboard where it lived in a wooden box with other small toys. I never spoke of this to anyone in my family.

(174–5) The "flooded ruins of a king's palace" refers to the Minoan palace of Zakros in the southeast corner of Crete. Through seismic action Crete has, within historic time, tilted and, while at the western end the former tide mark can be seen on the cliffs well above present sea level, the eastern end has sunk and some of the excavated rooms at Zakros are not only well below the current ground level, but also below the water table. The final, italicized words were spoken to Joseph in Egypt, after the death of Herod, by an angel in a dream: "Arise, and take the young child and his mother, and go into the land of Israel: for they are dead which sought the young child's life" (Matthew 2.19–20).

175. An old man at Midnight Mass

"Midnight Mass" usually refers, as here, to the service commonly held in Catholic and Anglican churches around midnight on Christmas Eve. The location I had in mind for this poem was a particular isolated country church in Herefordshire, but "familiar outhouse" links it to the stable or cowshed in Bethlehem implied as the birthplace of Jesus at Luke 2.7: "And she [Mary] brought forth her firstborn son and wrapped him in swaddling clothes, and laid him in a manger; because there was no room for them in the inn." The "morsel [...] of the broken body of life" refers to the communion wafer, on the basis of the earliest surviving account of the Last Supper, written by Paul, which is incorporated in the prayer of Consecration in the Catholic Mass or Anglican Holy Communion: "the Lord Jesus in the same night that he was betrayed took bread: And when he had given thanks, he brake it and said, Take, eat: this is my body which is broken for you" (I Corinthians 11.24–25) — taken with Jesus' statements "I am the resurrection and the life" and "I am the way, the truth and the life" (John 11.25, and 14.6). The "star point of clarity" alludes to the star which guided the Magi to the "midwinter birth" in Bethlehem: "the star, which they saw in the east, went before them, till it came and stood over the place where the young child was" (Matthew 2.9).

176–178. A Brief Guide to the Monastery of Daphni
(176) The monastery of Daphni is situated on the western edge of Athens on the road to Corinth. The "drum" is an architectural feature, a squat cylinder which supports a dome and is itself supported on columns, arches and squinches below.

(177) In Jesus' so-called *parable* of the sheep and the goats (really a prophecy based on a simile), he says that on the day of judgement the "son of man" (by which he is unerstood to be referring to himself), when "all the nations" are gathered before him, "shall separate the one from another, as a shepherd divideth his sheep from his goats: And he shall set the sheep on his right, but the goats on the left", and the goats are those who "shall go away into everlasting punishment" (Matthew 25.31–33, 45). "Pantocrator" is the equivalent of "Almighty", and the icon of the Pantocrator represents Christ in majesty, but also, usually, Christ in judgement. It is commonly found, as at Daphni, occupying the central dome of an Orthodox church. Jesus is thought to have been around 30 years old when he was crucified (hence "his thirty mortal

years"). In the Gospel of John, Jesus says not only "I and the Father are one" (10.30) but also "he that hath seen me hath seen the Father" (14.9). "Gentle Jesus" is a phrase best known from Charles Wesley's hymn for children that begins "Gentle Jesus, meek an mild, / Look upon a little child". Holman Hunt's well-known painting of Jesus with the crown of thorns and a halo is "the pained and caring white-robed Christ with gothic lantern in his hand"; it illustrates Revelation 3.20: "Behold, I stand at the door and knock: if any man hear my voice, and open the door, I will come in to him."

(178) "The book he holds" refers to the "book of life", referred to four times in the Book of Revelation, most pertinently in a vision of the Last Judgement: "And I saw a great white throne, and him that sat on it, from whose face the earth and heaven fled away [...] And I saw the dead, small and great, stand before God; and the books were opened: and another book which is the book of life: and the dead were judged out of those things which were written in the books, according to their works. [...] And whosoever was not found written in the book of life was cast into the lake of fire" (Revelation 20. 11–15).

179–181. To the Ayatolla Khomeini

Throughout the poem, words in double quotation marks are from the translation of the Ayatolla's speech published at the time in *The Guardian*.

(179) The Iranian date the 3rd of Esfand 1367 corresponds to the 11th of February 1989. The Ayatolla died on the 3rd of June 1989. The phrase "the slaughter-house of love" may be traced (though I did not know it when I wrote this poem in 1989) to the thirteenth-century Persian poet Jalal ad-Din Muhammad Rumi:

> In the slaughterhouse of love they kill only the best, none of the weak or deformed. Don't run away from this dying. Whoever's not killed for love is dead meat.

The phrase doesn't seem, as I had once supposed, to be of Quranic origin. Salman Rushdie's novel *The Satanic Verses* was first published in 1988. A *fatwa* issued by the Ayatollah on the 14th of February 1989, condemning Rushdie to death, was followed by several assassination attempts; the novelist was given police protection in the UK and lived in hiding for the next nine years. Copies of his book were publicly burned in several countries, including the UK. The dust jacket of the original hardback edition had on the spine (and also, rather larger, on the front) a detail from a 17th-century Indian painting of "Rustam killing the White Demon" (in the Victoria and Albert Museum, London).

(180–181) Words in italics in the last three paragraphs are from N. J. Dawood's translation of *The Koran* published by Penguin.

182–183. Ite missa est

(182) There is no consensus on the original meaning of *Ite missa est*, the ancient formula of dismissal at the end of the Latin Mass. It is often rendered in English, as "Go, the mass is ended", as here at the end of the poem, but this cannot really be correct. "Mass" derives from the noun *missa*, a variant of *missio*, meaning a "sending forth" or "dismissal". "Go, it is the dismissal" is, therefore, possible. But *missa* may in this case be a past participle (feminine singular) of the verb *mitto* (send, dismiss), implying some feminine noun which "is dismissed", such as the *ecclesia* or congregation. According to the doctrine of the Real Presence of Christ in the "Elements" (bread and wine) of the Mass, at the moment of consecration (the repetition of Jesus' words at the Last Supper, "this is my body" etc.), although the appearance of the bread and wine remains unchanged, their essential nature is transformed into the body and blood of Christ. The "Sanctuary" is the part of a church containing the altar (here called "Table"); and "where guilded pillars raised a canopy above the Table" describes an architecturural feature of, but by no means unique to, Huddersfield Parish Church (St Peter's in the town centre). "Token" refers to the communion wafer; "Cup" to the chalice which holds the consecrated wine ("cup" is the usual English translation of the Greek word *potêrion* in the relevant New Testament texts). I cannot now find the justification for the water which has washed the "Cup" being "poured into the footings of the House", but I think I must once have read of this practice, which I associated with the presence of small drain holes in the bases of recesses in the walls of certain churches, located close to the altar, in which the vessels used in the Mass are placed. "House" is used here and below to mean "church", a "house of God". I use "immaculate conceptions" in a literal sense, unconnected with the doctrine of the Immaculate Conception, which is often confused with the Virgin Birth (of Jesus) but refers to the belief that by special divine dispensation Mary the mother of Jesus, alone of all mortals, was born without the stain of Original Sin (the sin of Adam and Eve in the Garden of Eden supposedly transmitted to all their descendants, that is, the whole of humanity). Although the idea of the Immaculate Conception dates back to the fourth century it was only proclaimed as a *dogma* (necessary element of belief for Catholics) in 1854. "Host" is derived from Latin *hostia* meaning a sacrificial victim and refers to the bread which is regarded as the body of the sacrificed Jesus. In Catholic and High Anglican churches fragments of the consecrated bread may be "reserved" for veneration or for the communion of the sick, in a small cupboard with a door, often placed on the altar, or forming a integral part of the structure of the altarpiece behind; this is known as "the Tabernacle". In view of the doctrine of the Real Presence, Jesus at the Last Supper (which is re-enacted in the Mass) distributed his own body and blood to the disciples, hence "self-dispensed at the Feast".

(183) "Deposition" is a technical (especially art-historical) term for the taking down of Jesus from the Cross. Here it is a question not of the actual Crucifixion but of the large crucifix (or "rood") which often surmounts the "rood screen" (here just "the Screen") where it is present in a church, separating the chancel from the nave (where the congregation sit); and "Deposition of the Flesh" here supposes the removal of the flesh of a plaster or wooden representation of the body of Christ on the Cross, to reveal, as in the succeeding lines, a skeleton still held to the Cross by nails or "iron spikes". And "an ironic Superscription" refers to the account of the Crucifixion in the Gospel of Luke (with parallels in the other three Gospels): "And a superscription was also written over him in letters of Greek, and Latin, and Hebrew, THIS IS THE KING OF THE JEWS" (Luke 24.38). It was evidently written on the instructions of Pilate, the Roman governor (procurator) of Judea who had, somewhat reluctantly, obliged the Jewish authorities by condemning Jesus to death. They then complained to Pilate saying, "Write not, The King of the Jews, but that he said, I am the King of the Jews", to which Pilate memorably replied "What I have written I have written" (John 19.21–22).

184–185. That other city

Dreyck Dyne was my therapist in London at critical times in the 1980s. He died in 1999, but this poem was written some years before that. The epigraph is from the first stanza of Cavafy's poem "The city", in which the speaker of the poem quotes back to another person that person's own words; in the second stanza he proceeds to disabuse the other of his expectations of escape: "No new places will you find [...] the city will follow you." The "other city" that I had in mind was Alexandria, the presumed city of Cavafy's poem, but more significantly here the Alexandria of Lawrence Durrell's *The Alexandria Quartet*, and particularly the scene in Mnemjian's barber shop at the start of Chapter II of *Balthzar* (pp. 24–28, first edition) — the barber shop where various characters regularly met in the mornings to be shaved (hence "if you would go without your beard"). Durrell's fictional scene has to be dated to the mid 1930s (hence "in some other time"). The "next stage of our liturgy... where what is... is broken" refers both to the communion service ("the Liturgy" in the Orthodox Church) — see the note to p. 175 ("An old man at midnight mass") — and also to the breaking and reshaping of psychic structures through therapy.

185. Pins and needles

The question of how many angels could dance on the head of a pin was probably not a real medieval debate, but a seventeenth-century Protestant coinage to satirize the complex minutiae of certain strands of medieval scholastic theology. The attempt "to produce a smaller camel" alludes to the saying of Jesus: "It is easier for a camel to go through the eye of a needle, than for a rich man to enter the kingdom of God" (Matthew 19.24). With "needles dwarfing Cleopatra's" I had in mind space rockets; and some of the super-rich still fondly imagine they might escape to another planet, once this one is completely wrecked. "Cleopatra's Needle" can refer to any of three Egyptian stone obelisks taken to London, Paris and New York in the nineteenth century (though less often to the one in Paris). They all date from well over a thousand years before the time of the famous Cleopatra, Cleopatra VII, of Shakespeare's *Antony and Cleopatra*. The one in London stands beside the Thames on the Victoria Embankment; it is 21 metres high.

186. Preaching with precaution
The background to this poem is the much-illustrated theme of Francis of Assisi preaching to the birds.

186. Veni creator spiritus
The title is the opening of a Latin hymn; one English translation begins "Come, Holy Ghost, our hearts inspire", but more accurately the title is "come, creator–spirit". "Spirit" – "inspire" – "breath" and "breathe".

189–192. A hotel room in Chania
Chania is large port town on the north coast of Crete, towards the western end. It was the capital of island until 1971 when that title was transferred to Iraklio (Herakleion).

(190) The 28th of October is *Ochi* Day in Greece (*Ochi* = No), a national holiday and a time for military parades. It marks the anniversary of the day in 1940 when the Greek dictator Ioannis Metaxas refused Mussolini's demand for free passage of Italian troops through Greece, supposedly in a one-word telegram: OCHI.

(191) Athenagoras I (1886–1972), a US citizen, was the Ecumenical Patriarch of the Orthodox Church, that is, the Patriarch of Constantinople (Istanbul) from 1948 until his death. The church in Crete has never been part of the autocephalous Orthodox Church of Greece, but has always remained directly under the authority of the Ecumenical Patriarch.

193. Dramatic fragment
The italicized words in line 4 are from T. S. Eliot, *The Waste Land*, III: "The Fire Sermon", where Tiresias, the blind seer from Sophocles *Oedipus the king* and other Greek tragedies, observes the seduction of a typist by a house agent's clerk.

197–198. Behind the Veil
(197) "The sun is covered by the moon […] the moon lets go her grip upon the sun" — three of the four Gospels describe what sounds like a solar eclipse on the afternoon of the Crucifixion: "And when the sixth hour was come, there was darkness over the whole land until the ninth hour (Mark 15.33, compare Matthew 27.45 and Luke 23.44). "Son,

forsaken by the father" derives from Jesus' cry from the cross "at the ninth hour", "Eloi, Eloi, lama sabachthani? which is, being interpreted, My God, My God, why hast thou forsaken me?" (Mark 15.34, with a close parallel at Matthew 27.46). Jesus' last cry immediately preceding his death on the Cross is "wordless" at Mark 15.37 and Matthew 27.50, but given words in the other Gospels: "Father, into they hands I commend my spirit" (Luke 23.46), and "It is finished" (John 19.30). In both Mark and Matthew the final wordless cry is immediately followed by "And behold the veil of the temple was rent in twain from the top to the bottom" ("behold" in Matthew only). The "holiest place" refers to the most sacred space in the Jerusalem Temple, the "Holy of Holies", where God was thought to be present among his people. Surrounded by a heavy curtain ("the Veil") supported on pillars, it was entered only once a year by the High Priest, on the Day of Atonement. In Solomon's Temple, the Holy of Holies housed the Ark of the Covenant, a chest containing — biblical accounts differ — the original scrolls of the Ten Commandments and/or various artifacts associated with Moses and Aaron. The "Mercy Seat" was the gold cover of the Ark which had golden statues of Cherubim at either side. A part of the annual ritual involved the High Priest sprinkling the Mercy Seat with the blood of a sacrificial animal. With the destruction of the First (or Solomon's) Temple by the Babylonians in 587 BC the Ark and the Mercy Seat disappeared. In the Second Temple, constructed in the late 6th century BC and destroyed by the Romans in AD 70, the Holy of Holies was probably empty. The woman/goddess in the poem menstruating on the Mercy Seat will no doubt seem a blasphemous affront to adherents of the patriarchal religions, in which women are seen as spiritually inferior, and indeed ritually unclean at times of childbirth and menstruation. The injunction "put off that cloak of impotence, / those robes of mourning" echoes Baruch 1.5: "Put off, O Jeruslaem, the garments of mourning and affliction." Baruch is one of the books of the Apocrypha which were included, between Old and New Testaments, in the original 1611 edition of the Authorized Version of the Bible, but are generally omitted from modern editions.

(198) The last line of the poem goes back to Matthew, where, immediately after the rending of the Veil, we find "and the earth did quake, and the rocks rent; and the graves were opened; and many bodies of the saints arose, and came out of the graves after his resurrection, and went into the holy city and appeared to many" (27.51–53). If there was indeed a rumour, picked up by the author of Matthew or his sources, that such a thing happened, we may discount the improbable lapse of time (some 36 hours) between the graves opening and the saints emerging from their graves "*after* [Jesus'] resurrection" as a theological nicety — Jesus must have been raised from the dead before others could be — and restore the rumour to the evening of the Crucifixion.

198. Good Friday in Herakleion

"Great Preparation" translates the Greek phrase *Megali Paraskevi*. The Greek names of the days of the week, with the exception of "Lord's Day" (Sunday) are based on the Jewish names and "Friday" is *Paraskevi*, the Jewish "[Day of] Preparation", preparation, that is, for the Sabbath, the Jewish Holy Day. *Megali Paraskevi* could — indeed often is — translated as "Great Friday". As for the Tree of Life, in the biblical account of Creation we read, "the Lord God planted a garden eastward in Eden [...] and out of the ground made the Lord God to grow every tree that is pleasant to the sight and good for food; the tree of life also in the midst of the garden, and the tree of the knowledge of good and evil" (Geneisis 2.8–9). Adam was explicitly commanded not to eat from the latter tree, but the "tree of life" is not mentioned again until Adam and Eve are expelled from the Garden of Eden: "And the Lord God said, Behold, the man is become as one of us, to know both good and evil, and now, lest he put forth his hand, and take also of the tree of life, and eat, and live for ever [...] So he drove out the man; and he placed at the east of the garden of Eden Cherubims, and a flaming sword which turned every way, to keep the way of the tree of life" (Genesis 3.22–24 — not one of the best bits of translation in the Authorized Version, with God's uncompleted sentence and the double plural "Cherubims"). In the poem, "the Scarecrow" (Christ on the Cross) has taken on the role of the Cherubim and the flaming sword, "to keep the sparrows [the schoolgirls in the procession and the rest of humanity] from the Tree of Life". The second paragraph describes an example of the Orthodox processon of the *epitaphios* on the afternoon or evening of Good Friday. The *epitaphios* is a covered bier (which may be simple or extremely elaborate) in which is laid a recumbent statue or other representation of the dead Christ. Very often the statue is approximately half life-size ("too small by half").

200. Holy Saturday

The day between Good Friday and Easter Sunday is often called Holy Saturday, or Great Saturday in the Orthodox Church. It is, in the Christian myth, the only full day of Jesus' death and descent into Hell (to rescue Adam and the rest of the worthy deceased). The last paragraph returns to some of those involved in the death of Jesus. When Jesus was brought before him, the Roman governor, Pontius Pilate, wanted to release him because he "found no fault in this man" (Luke 23.14). There was a custom at the Feast of Passover that the governor should release one prisoner to be selected by the Jewish people in Jeruslem. Pilate proposed to release Jesus but the crowd shouted instead for Barabbas, who is said in one Gospel to have been imprisoned "for a certain sedition made in the city, and for murder" (Luke 23.19, compare Mark 15.7). In Matthew he is only "a notable prisoner" (27.16), but John (18.40) states clearly and simply, "Barabbas was a robber" (hence those who "preferred the thief"). Those who "shouted for blood" are the same crowd, who said of Jesus "His blood be on us, and on our children" (Matthew 27.24). Nails as such are not mentioned in the Gospel accounts of the Crucifixion, but this cruel method of slow execution involved fixing the condemned man to a wooden cross with nails or iron spikes driven through between the bones of the wrists and ankles (not through the palms of the hands and the equivalent part of the feet as in most Christian images — that simply could not have worked). Those "who drove the nails" would have been Roman soldiers, and it was one of them who "forced the spear in under the ribs": in order to satisfy the Jews and get the bodies of Jesus and the two thieves crucified with him down from the crosses before the start of the Sabbath, at sunset on that day, the soldiers came to break their legs (which would have caused the bodies to slump putting intense pressure on the lungs, leading quickly to asphyxiation), "But when they came to Jesus, and saw that he was already dead, they brake not his legs: but one of the soldiers with a spear pierced his side, and forthwith came there out blood and water" (John 19.33–34).

201. Easter Vigil

On "Holy Saturday", see the previous note. The expression "naked as
the Risen Christ" may seem surprising, but nakedness is clearly implied
by the account of the Resurrection in the Gospel of John (20.1–7),
where Mary Magdalene, having found the tomb empty, ran to "Simon
Peter and the other disciple, the one whom Jesus loved [John]", and
told them "they have taken the Lord from the tomb"; the two disciples
ran to the tomb, but John got there first "and stooping to look in, he
saw the linen cloths lying there, but he did not go in. Then Simon Peter
came, following him, and went into the tomb; he saw the linen cloths
lying, and the napkin, which had been on his head, not lying with the
linen cloths but rolled up in a place by itself." There are two statues by
Michelangelo of the Risen Christ entirely naked. Many other works of
art depict Christ loosely draped in the grave cloths, in direct contra-
diction of John (and no other Gospel mentions the "linen cloths" at
all). There are a number of wonderful paintings by Van Gogh depicting
orchards with their spring blossoms. The expression "crows —
migrated from a darker canvas" refers to Van Gogh's painting
"Wheatfield with crows", one of his last paintings done in July 1890.
This wheatfield was the location of his attempted suicide on the 27th of
July. He tried to shoot himself through the heart but missed, though he
died some days later from his wound.

202–204. Cracks and hollows in the Rock of Ages

"Rock of Ages" is not a biblical phrase, though there are many
metaphorical references to God as a "rock" in the Bible; it belongs to
an eighteenth-century hymn by Augustus Toplady which begins and
ends, "Rock of Ages, cleft for me, / Let me hide myself in thee."
(202) The italicized words in the first paragraph of the poem come
from Revelation 1.9-10. Rorschach tests are used to assess the
psychological state of persons presenting symptoms of mental illness.
They are sheets which look as if they were formed by spilling ink on a
sheet of paper and folding it in half, the resulting random shapes
having bilateral symmetry about a vertical centre line. Persons being
assessed are required to look at a series of these and describe what the
"inkblots" suggest to them.
(203) The "fissure in the rock from which God spoke" has no

scriptural basis but is part of the traditional understanding of the Cave of Apocalypse close to the Monastery of Saint John on the island of Patmos: in fact a triple fissure said to represent the Trinity. The italicized words in the first paragraph on this page are from Revelation 1.11. In late 1922 after the defeat of Greek forces in Asia Minor by the new Turkish army of Mustafa Kemal (later known as Kemal Attaturk), most Greeks living in Asia Minor fled to Greece; others were forcibly moved to Greece in the negotiated exchange of populations between Greece and Turkey in 1923. John is believed to have been exiled to Patmos by the Romans, and much of the Book of Revelation can be read as a diatribe against Rome, equated with "that Great city Babyon, that mighty city" (Revelation 18.10) which is to be destroyed.

(204) Little is known of Prochoros, named once in the Bible as one of seven men chosen to assist the Apostles (Acts 6.5). His association with the author of Revelation as a co-exile with him in Patmos is little more than a speculative legend, but a tradition accepted by the Orthodox Church. The idea, in my words, of "Satan's armies [...] allowed [...] for a time to wreak God's wrath upon the earth" is not quite explicit in the Revelation, but a great deal of that book is about the destructive wrath of God and the various agencies which carry it out. See, for example, the opening of the seven seals by the Lamb (= Christ) in Chapter 6, where, as each of the first four seals are opened a horseman appears: the first "went forth conquering and to conquer" (6.2); the second was given power "to take peace from the earth so that they should kill one another" (6.4); and the fourth, named "Death and Hell", was given power "over the fourth part of the earth to kill with the sword" (6.8).

205. Sea voices
The epigraph consists of the opening words from each of the first three paragraphs of Lawrence Durrell's novel *Justine*, though I have placed the second one first.

206–209. The silence of the icons
The self-disparaging parenthetic subtitle "a periphrastic study . . ." is from T. S. Eliot, *Four Quartets*, "East Coker", II. In Eliot's usage, though, it refers back ("That was a way of putting it") to one of those wonderful passages in the *Four Quartets* where Eliot's imagination is

freed, briefly, from the fetters of abstract and religious ideas: "What is the late November doing / With the disturbance of the spring / And creatures of the summer heat / And snowdrops writhing under feet [...]?" My poem, however, is not similarly liberated. Much of the content of the poem grew out of my experiences and encounters when wandering alone (and often getting lost) in the mountains of North Wales and Crete in the 1970s and 80s.

INDEX OF TITLES AND FIRST LINES

Titles are in italic type, first lines upright. Where first lines are very short, all or part of the second line is added (and occasionally the third). Entries beginning with "A", "An" or "The" will be found under A and T, not under the first letter of the second word. Where, in the main text, poems have titles in Greek with the English in brackets afterwards, the English title is placed first in this Index. Alphabetization is by whole word, so that, for example "Rare the Greek village" precedes "Rarely in such places". Where there is a sequence of poems under the same title (such sequences contain from two to twenty poems), the first line of each of the constituent poems is given. In the text such poems are separated by the sign below.

A bitch straining at the leash, she scents the open sea	60
A Brief Guide to the Monastery of Daphni	176
A classical dichotomy	12
A fritillary, once brilliant black and orange	90
A hotel room in Chania	189
a hunt wihout nets (ἄλινος θήρα / alinos thera)	144
A kind of death	199
A minor accident some weeks ago	94
A mixed blessing	170
A mourning walk on a spring afternoon	31
A photograph perhaps . . . a mask, a portrait even	3
A royal dilemma	14
A spasm — long and shuddering	77
A timetrick	187

Above the west door of a city church	186
Aegean snapshots 7 x 5	60
After California / Belfast feels more empty	163
After the child, no more of me	113
After you / we return to a bed / ravaged	25
Air India to JFK	68
Alison + I	156

Alison + I = ailinos, / a plaintive dirge 156
Alison of Troy (Η Άλισον της Τροίας / I Álison tis Trías) 139
Also in sleep 140

An Antique Valentine 74
An die ferne Geliebte 87
An hour or more / of loitering in a Cornish lane 164
An isolated patch of cloud 61
An old man at midnight mass 175
An old recording 18
An' so I learn some home truths 163

And Bashō / the beginning lost in silence 38
and I, I lie alone 103
And is the village cross inscribed as well 114
and twelve months later 29
and two generations later 82
Anna Palaiologou's gate 30
Annunciation. Implantation of the seed 170
Anticipating spring 88
Ars is longa, vita's brevis 157
As I long 146
As I long for your heart to open 146
As I only noted cursorily at first 149
As in loving, so in Lagan's stream 141
As on lips I fixed my gaze 127
At an Oxford conference 21
At breakfast, two rabbits on the lawn 114
At India's breezy southern tip 66
At the Crater Lakes 109
Attic power cut 54
Autumn in Chania 85
Awake now, lying on my back, my hand in sleep 140

Baggage handling 161
Bashō, Oppenheimer, and a dream 33

Behind the Veil	197
Belfast. Thursday the twentieth of June	144
Beware, Dog is all the notice says	114
Birdsong and raucous laughter	58
Bodily comfort	78
Breaking the surface / of the antique / (Socratic) frog-pond	60
But even at the dress rehearsal	35
Butrint: the visit to the site and now	128
By the time we laid you here to rest	27
Capitals	110
Church (rems of) by the lake	118
Cloudscapes	70
Coincidence (1st of October 1991)	13
Confusion	188
Cracks and hollows in the Rock of Ages	202
Customs	161
Dawn ferry	59
Dead friends	16
Do we dare to summon you once more onto the stage	193
Doors, shutters open wide, curtains undrawn	89
Do'st harbour still within thine heart	74
Dramatic fragment	193
Dream after dream / lost	64
Durrell, living in the hills of Cyprus	26
Dusty tracks that run among untended olive groves	91
Easter vigil	201
Emerged from cramped and fitful sleep	87
Enter, if you have to, from the south	175
Escaped at last into what's left / of light and air and time	36
Everywhere I go, I thought	90
Exactly opposite my balcony and facing me	191
Familiar predicament	90

Five pairs of eyes inform the room   81
Flying the friendly skies   161
For a daughter born 12.45 a.m.   80
For nine months now the world has been without you   31
Forget all this is marble for a moment   6
Friend in despair   112
From the harbour (as Durrell would insist) / of Sycorax   127
From the Manickam Tourist Home   67

Ghosts   192
Gliders / turning so slowly in the air   117
Good Friday in Herakleion   198
Good Friday in Herakleion, Great Preparation / as they call it here   198
Grandma is dead. So we all / move up   82
Greek mariners or *The naming of craft*   10

Half a Cornish pasty in the mud   120
Hangovers   72
He came from a background of dust   194
He lies and moans. He sighs   112
He stood in the early hours in an empty street   186
Hearing the dawn   58
Here's to you, Ma!   27
Here you can watch / non-stop films from Hollywood   92
Hiroshima. Nagasaki. Twin stars of our birth   35
Holy Saturday   200
Homecomings   9
Hours pass warily, / staring at the table   104
Hypertension   94

I am not here. I am not here   188
I arrived with caseloads of hope   161
I can imagine with some pleasure   184
I can see him now / as I often saw him   7
I do not think that they will sing to me   57
I don't think March would have been / high season   118

I fight through a wasteland of twigs   121
I have read in translation a speech you delivered   179
I'm here to photograph the bust of Vlasis Gavrilidis   171
I only had that room three weeks   189
I picked up in the street today a bookmark   13
I saw her standing in the doorway opposite   57
I saw you born / in blood and water   80
I sensed she was there and reached out behind   78
I sit in a train / staring at your picture   151
I too have come to an island   205
I've often wondered in these past few days   191
I walk the backroads of my mind   115
I was in the isle called Patmos / and on the Lord's day too   202
I wept when I saw the children in the street   192

Idling on your deck / in warm midday sun   159

In a solitary deck chair   159
In memoriam L.G.D.   26
In other years they will be green again   11
In Salonica today the sea   20
In so late an hour   142
In solaria   150
In the Commonwealth Cemetery at Souda   23
In the harbour's clear green water, fish, neatly segregated   60
In the Lady Chapel at Ely   75
In these four nights in your small house   158

Inside my head three pairs of feet   72
Ionian Sea (ἇλς ἰόνιος / hals ionios)   126
Is an old Muse any less inspiring?   129
It's early morning, and a dog / is barking   70
It was, I realize now, the first moment   130
Ite missa est   182

July the first, and, inevitably, I'm remembering   149
Just past the old bus terminus   46

Ka and Kavafis   42
Kalliopi's recent coat of bright red paint   129
Kampala — city of more hills / than Rome   110
Klafthmonos Square, Athens, 25th of March 2001   171

Lady Julian's offering   166
Last night our last lost opportunity   137
Late evening after sun-scorched August day   34
Later, on a narrower road, I find   41
Leave in the fog. Visibility low   162
Lidl's been delayed it seems   29
Lies sleepless in a concrete barn   201
Light from water / on the bows of resting boats   60
Like a lioness, like a lion (Σα λιόντισσα, σα λιοντάρι /
        Sa lióndissa, sa liondári)   138
Lilies of the valley   79
Little deaths   77
Loans I never could repay   158
Loins and eyes   125
London winter evening: linked verse   104
Long ago   82
Long dusty road   110
Love is a verb without a future tense   95
Lunch on Poros   55

Made of marble (Λάϊνος / Laïnos)   135
Mahoma Falls   108
Man losing his bearings   162
Memorials (1941, 1989)   39
Minoan royal prerogative   84
Minutes before it reached him / the poet Ka   42
Monastic silences in Kefalonia   71
Moored side by side on the beach   59
Mouse poem for a child   83
Moving among man-planted planes   99

Murder dead loves' ghosts   79
My pack and clothes / in various shades   116

Next time I come   161
Night conceits   53
Night out on Thasos   54
Nightmare   113
No aisle for Alison?   155
No hearse, no tall black hats, no stiff attire   9
Not just the room but all the square / below the balcony   190
Now we have kissed   131
Now, with the birth of a granddaughter   82

O Snail!   131
On its back in the gutter / where the road crosses   114
On Noah's Ark, where they were waiting for a branch   138
On the morning of the day he died   24
Once again, after long absence   175
Once he called it "sweet" / that thing he'd had a hand in making   34
One version of my life died in that room   192
Our dawn descent to the lake   109

Past midnight when we left the table   132
Peering down midflight through scattered cloud   70
Pins and needles   185
Plateia Varnava, Athens   96
Platonic manikins, Athens   93
Poem for the countryside — impossible now   119
Poison on Poros   15
Preaching with precaution   186
Preparations   111
Princeton porches   69
Princeton's a lovely place   69
Proved February's only cloudless day   88

Rare the Greek village without its war memorial   19

Rarely in such places do the bones / have names 14
Remember me to him 81
Returning with his fellows from a morning's sport 84
Riding at anchor 59

's I alone again? 147
Safari drive, Uganda 107
Sail on from Bougainvillea 130
Saloon (Σαλόνι / Salóni) 137
Saturday night and Sunday morning 56
Scarcely ruffled in the August dawn 61
Sea voices 205
Security 161
Seems a comfortless place to lie in 27
Sleeping, not leaping 89
So in Albania 128
So many marble heads without their bodies 12
So nail your courage to the sticking place 132
So this is the station where we'd planned to arrive 73
Someone is stroking my head / with a cricket bat 72
Something like the ghost of a rabbit 117
Speculum, speculum or *In my Lady's Chamber* 75
Springfield (optimistic name) Road, Cambridge 143
Still life, Sigh . . . gone 22
Strange land: a child's story 173
Stretched on the lime-trees of night he dreams 199
Sun and Sunday morning 115

Thanks, then, to Mister Cavafy, who sailed this sea 126
That afternoon 7
That other city 184

The babe leaped in her womb, she thought, for joy 172
The Barn Farm Shop / offers 120
The bedside table: a candle / and a quartz alarm clock 103
The beginning lost in silence 33

The big blue Atlantic / pock-marked with white	68
The brains of giraffes / are too far above the ground	107
The bus from Galatas was packed	106
The difficult syntax of love	95
The dog had barked at my arrival, but the sign	71
The effects of alcohol	25
The eye, though it sport no accoutrements of gender	125
The family plot, Salendine Nook Baptist Cemetery	46
The German monument, the Blue Guide Crete / asserts	39
The hands of God	169
The heroes, gods and goddesses	10
The Ho Chi Minh City Museum now	22
The huge, turf-cut cross of yellowish chalk	117
The journey to Asine	106
The journeys of Holy Saturday	200
The Lady Julian of Norwich, whom I heard discussed	166
The Lagan flows a hundred metres off	141
The last breakfast	24
The lost time weighs on me as though	33
The military of course held all performing rights	35
The Muse was prescient	124
The noisy flapping of the last few crows	54
The other ring (the one you didn't buy)	155
The Pilgrims' Way (postcards from Kent)	114
The planet shrinks and wingless angels multiply	185
The quick and the dead	101
The railway station in Kampala	73
The road along the crater rim	109
The secret beach	11
The sick house	194
The silence of the icons	206
The sort of gravestone that might well	86
The square is named for Barnabas, Saint Barnabas	96
The sun is covered by the moon	197
The surface of the earth is hard and cold	65
The swallows of Kastoria	99

The view from the northside balconies   67

Theatre of Dionysus, Athens   6
Then suddenly it was cold   85
There is no laptop here   143
There's only one way / from one day to the next   187
There was a mouse who had no tale   83
These frozen and idealized forms   93
These places   91
This is a long-distance call   164
This morning there's no message from you   147
This time yesterday / I was talking to you in your bed   150
This winter-lunchtime seafront restaurant   55
Three strides and you're home   111
Thunder without rain; and voices   21
Tired from a night flight, and ill, unable   59
To the Ayatollah Khomeini : an oblique tribute   179
Tomb of Antipatros, a Macedonian   86
Tonight I don't think I shall sleep at all   142
Tonight I'm eating on the pavement, opposite   30
Tonight, reading Electra / fails to electrify   54
Too many kissing-gates / on Footpath two-one-three   116
Travails on arrival and departure   161
Travelling alone   90
TV in Vietnam in 2012   92
Twice the stars it takes to plough the sky   61
Two caryatids supporting / just inside the garden gate   115
Two hundred miles on trains / a damp November day   3
Two tall trees stand / side by side at the water's edge   109
Two, three hours in the heat   23

United — well, yes and no   161
Unspoken   193
update on redevelopment (February 2019) with automotive digressions   27

Vast tree stripped bare   110

Veni creator spiritus   186
Visitation   172
Visitors   66
Volcano days   65

Wake / in a hot and strangely patterned room   64
Waking from dreams   64
Waking, midday, on a river bank   64
War dead   19
Was it weeks or months since I had seen you   62
We arrive too late, to find   101
We die; the store of our experience is dispersed   157
We have the words / but only they the knowledge   193
We meet / across a coffin   16
We met (auspiciously perhaps for future voyaging)   139
We reach the village with no problem   108
We're all in the hands of God, you say   193
We sat on a park bench   135
Well, Geoff, what d'you think of married life?   18
What is a life when you lie in the dark   56
When I arrived, one day years ago   62
When the icons no longer spoke to us   206
Whose is this unwashed marble face   15
Whosoever thou art that enterest this church   119
With the lower slopes enveloped   70
Words don't really exist. They're all in the mind   120

Years later, after he'd been investigated   37
Years later / after many more   17
Yes, through all the world I seek for you (Ναι, σ' όλο τον κόσμο
      σε γυρεύω / Nai, s' ólo ton kósmo se yirévo)   151
Yesterday the sea was glittering, inviting   20
You have shadowed me, O Christ   182
You took me away to a strange land   173
You turn away to seek your other lover — Sleep   53
Your scan detected / prohibited items   161

Lightning Source UK Ltd.
Milton Keynes UK
UKHW041120301120
374347UK00001B/37